PARENTS and ADOLESCENTS Living Together

PART 2: Family Problem Solving

Marion S. Forgatch
Gerald R. Patterson

2nd EDITION

Research Press
2612 North Mattis Avenue
Champaign, Illinois 61822

(800) 519-2707
www.researchpress.com

To Patti Chamberlain and Kate Kavanagh, friends and colleagues with whom we have grown as clinicians over the years, and to John Reid, who continues to guide our therapy

Contents

Acknowledgments

This book and its companion, *Part 1: The Basics,* would never have been written without the gentle persuasion and persistant encouragement of Scot Patterson. As the original editor and publisher of these books, as well as in his role as family member, he has given these books their life force. As in the first volume, his contributions have been so extensive that the lines between authors and editor are blurred.

We have learned about the adventures involved in raising adolescents from a wide variety of families—our own, those of our friends, and the hundreds of families with problems who have sought help at the Oregon Social Learning Center. Their identities have been protected by changing circumstances, details, and names, but their experiences provide the underpinnings of the material.

We gratefully acknowledge the two decades of support for the research underlying the principles described. The National Institute of Mental Health sections on crime and delinquency, and mood, anxiety, and personality disorders have provided grants making it possible to work through many of the complicated problems inherent in the study and treatment of families.

The contributions of Margo Moore must also be acknowledged. She is much appreciated for providing uncomplaining and expert management of the manuscript both in its production and in the taming of the word processor throughout the numerous drafts of this book.

Finally, we would like to thank our clinical colleagues: John Reid, Patricia Chamberlain, Kate Kavanagh, and Thomas Dishion. Each of them has contributed knowledge of family therapy to the thinking reflected in this book. They are currently producing new materials for parents and professionals that will build on the treatment procedures that have been developed at OSLC. Our thanks also to Will Mayer for allowing us to use his cartoon ideas.

This book is neither the first or last word on the subject of family change. Rather, it describes a set of ideas that are in passage.

Preface

This book has been written to help parents manage the problems they typically encounter when their children reach adolescence. Even parents who have had very little trouble raising their children find that new problems arise during the teenage years. This is a difficult time for parents, and for children as well. It is a transition period when children go through rapid changes. Adolescents are no longer children, and yet they aren't quite adults. They alternate between expressing their own individuality and being dependent on their parents.

They can drive cars and demand increasing degrees of freedom. Parties are no longer a time for simple games and talking—now there is drinking and the use of drugs to contend with. Access to the Internet can expose adolescents to influences that are not in keeping with parental values. These experiences are difficult to handle, and parents often become concerned about their adolescents' ability to make wise choices. Parents living with adolescents are confronted with new issues on a regular basis, and these issues must be "negotiated" with adolescents instead of being decided by parents.

One of the most difficult challenges is striking a balance between protecting adolescents from serious trouble and giving them enough freedom to try out new experiences. Parents need effective techniques for producing lasting changes in adolescent problem behaviors, as well as ways to control the negative emotions that often accompany the struggles between parents and teenagers. Our research has shown that there are right ways and wrong ways to help adolescents change. The techniques outlined in this book are designed to teach parents the skills they need to maintain this balance without turning their households into battlegrounds.

This book draws on our experience as parents, researchers, and family therapists. Between us we have raised five children, all of whom are now beyond their adolescent years. We are also researchers who have devoted our professional careers to studying families (45 years for Jerry, 30 for Marion). Our work has focused on building a comprehensive framework for understanding the processes that operate within families, and helping troubled families change. The results of our studies, and those of our colleagues doing similar work, have been discussed in professional books and journals, but most of the concepts are not available to parents. Although there are hundreds of books written for parents, this is the only program that is based on modern coercion theory.

Both of us are members of the Oregon Social Learning Center (OSLC), which is a research facility staffed by a group of scientists and therapists who are dedicated to strengthening the American family. The decades of studies carried out at OSLC are unique in that they are concerned with real families who are dealing with problems and situations very much like yours. The purpose of this research is to design treatment approaches for families whose problems have gotten out of control. This blend of science and therapy has many practical implications for families. Our research indicates, for example, that parents in nondistressed families have specific family management skills that parents in disrupted families don't seem to have. When we teach these family management skills to parents who are having difficulties with their teenagers, problem behaviors decrease dramatically. The two books in the

Parents and Adolescents Living Together mini-series describe these family management principles in detail.

Our research at OSLC has involved thousands of families with children ranging in age from toddlers to adolescents. We have studied all kinds of families: "intact families," where the father and mother are the biological parents of the children; "stepfamilies," where there are two parents, only one of whom is a biological parent of the children; "blended families," where both parents in the family have children from previous relationships; "adoptive families," where the parents adopt children; and "single-parent families," where the children live with only one of their parents (often the mother), usually as the result of separation or divorce.

During the past three decades, social learning researchers have spent hundreds of thousands of hours conducting field studies in homes and classrooms across the country. What is being studied is the simple idea that people change as a result of the interactions they have on a daily basis with one another. Before these studies were undertaken, it was almost always assumed that interactions changed people, but no one could figure out just how this phenomenon worked, or even how to study it. For some reason it took social scientists a long time to come up with the idea of going into the real world to see what is going on in family life.

In our studies, we examine the family from many different perspectives: We ask parents and children (separately) about their experiences; we go into homes and observe the behavior of family members as they interact with one another; we call parents and children on the telephone and ask them what is happening on a daily basis; in the laboratory, we ask families to sit down and talk about their problems, and we study how they do that; we ask teachers to tell us how children behave in the school, and we talk to these children's classmates as well. The families involved in our research studies share large portions of their family life with us. The information in this book is based on these studies.

The clinical work at OSLC focuses on changing antisocial and aggressive behavior in children. This work covers a wide range of problem behaviors such as disobedience, arguing, tantrums, school problems, fighting, lying, stealing, shoplifting, burglary, assault, truancy, and substance abuse. Helping families with extreme problems has made it easier for us to see the processes that disrupt families because they are more dramatic. We have found that the best way to help adolescents with the problem behaviors mentioned here is to teach their parents how to change behavior. This almost always involves changing the parents' behavior as well as the adolescents'.

Some parents are disappointed when they find out how much effort it takes to make the necessary changes; they would rather have a professional do it for them, magically and with ease. Unfortunately, that plan doesn't work. Parents are in the best position to help their adolescents because parents control the resources that motivate them. Parents also determine whether the family environment is constructive and healthy. Perhaps the most important reason that parents are in the best position to help is that they are the ones who love their children enough to make the commitment necessary to socialize them and protect them from harmful experiences. For these reasons, it is necessary for parents to be actively involved in changing problematic adolescent behaviors.

The general approach in this book is to teach parents how to be consistent in applying commonsense techniques. If the problems your family is experiencing are relatively mild, this book should provide the information you need to smooth out the rough edges. If the problems involve long-standing or intensely angry struggles with one another, however, your family may not be able to change what is going on simply by reading this book. In that case, you should seek out a counselor, a psychologist, or a professional family therapist to help you make some of the necessary changes. It is very difficult for parents in severely distressed families to turn things around without some professional assistance and support. Parents of children diagnosed with AD/HD or other similar disorders also will need professional help if they are to be successful in using the techniques in this book.

Parenting can be incredibly rewarding when everything is going well, but it can be intensely frustrating and demoralizing when things get out of hand. We hope you can use the information in this book to make your family living experience one that is filled with love, joy, mutual respect, and a spirit of cooperation.

How to Use This Book

Although the skills presented in this book are based on common sense, it may take some practice to use them correctly. So that you can avoid critical pitfalls, we talk about the mistakes parents often make. Many of the common problems reported to us in therapy sessions are used as examples. Chapters 2–6 also include some "teaching dramas," which describe families "doing it right" and "doing it wrong." The characters and the situations are based on the families we have been in contact with—our own, our friends', and our clients'. The names and many of the details have been changed.

Parents who are using this book on their own should work through the chapters one at a time. We think it is best for you to read through the chapters in the order they are presented, but if your family circumstances are so dire that you need something to use right away, you might want to start by reading Chapter 6, on discipline. Each chapter ends with a homework assignment. These assignments are designed to help you put into practice the principles described in the chapter. The assignments build on one another, so it is important not to skip any of the chapters and to complete all the homework assignments.

Although we have tried to avoid using specialized language in this book, some psychological terms are difficult to avoid. Therefore, new terms are defined as they are introduced. For easy reference, a glossary appears at the back of the book. If you forget what a particular term means, simply flip back to the glossary for a quick reminder.

Use by Students and Professionals

Although it was mentioned earlier that the *Parents and Adolescents Living Together* mini-series is primarily for parents, it is also intended for psychology students and mental health professionals who want to understand coercion theory and parent management therapy. The material presented here is less technical than the information available in the professional literature, yet it provides a state-of-the-art understanding of important social learning concepts that is not available anywhere else. Students may find themselves reading this book as part of their course work in psychology, social work, or counseling programs. (It should be particularly revealing for younger students in that it presents the other side of the coin—that is, what it's like to be a parent.) This volume should also be very useful as an introduction to "social-interactional psychology," which is an exciting area of investigation and theory building.

About Part 2

Part 2 of the *Parents and Adolescents Living Together* miniseries builds on the skills developed in Part 1. In Part 2, the focus is on helping family members work together to resolve daily hassles and serious issues without getting angry. The book shows parents how to improve their communication and problem-solving skills, set up family meetings, and involve family members in solving problems. It carefully explains how parents can teach their adolescents to be responsible when it comes to schoolwork, sexual behavior, and drugs and alcohol; early warning signs of adolescent behavior problems and steps for intervention are clearly described. The approach is flexible so parents can develop a plan that reflects their own feelings about these critical issues.

INTRODUCTION

Problem Solving with Adolescents

Parents need to fortify their negotiation and problem-solving skills when their children become teenagers. Adolescence signals the beginning of a period of constant vigilance and prolonged stress for parents. The thunder of the next crisis can always be heard in the distance, and at any moment parents may find themselves in the center of another storm. The adolescent years are particularly worrisome for parents because their children have access to activities that could have serious consequences. Parents *should* be concerned about their teenagers driving cars, failing in school, and going to parties where alcohol and drugs may be present. The question is, how can you keep adolescents from getting into serious trouble when you aren't always there?

As parents, we know about the temptations our children face because we remember the things we did that gave our parents gray hair. Setting a new speed record in the family van, getting drunk at keggers, or "going all the way" may have seemed all right at the time, but in hindsight we can see that these activities were more risky than we realized. Every year, thousands of teenagers are injured or killed in senseless car accidents. Survey studies have shown that American adolescents are routinely exposed to alcohol and a wide variety of drugs. Research also indicates that our children are becoming sexually active at increasingly younger ages. This is particularly alarming in view of the fact that AIDS can be found in just about every community, and sexually transmitted diseases have reached almost epidemic proportions. In spite of these very real dangers, it is possible for teenagers to have fun with their peers without tragedy if they learn how to make good choices in tempting situations.

During the teenage years, parents need to watch for warning signs that their adolescents are experimenting with potentially harmful activities, and they need to know how to prevent problems from becoming serious when they suspect that something is going on. It is hard to monitor teenagers, however, because they are increasingly mobile and spend a considerable amount of time away from home. Testing the rules seems to be one of the mandates of adolescence, and teenagers also challenge whether the rules are *fair*. The question "Don't you trust me?" is heard all too often, at a time when parents know that they must be more observant than ever. Clearly, this is not the time to take a vacation from the rigors of setting rules, monitoring activities, imposing consequences, and solving problems.

This book provides step-by-step guidelines for negotiating sensitive issues and resolving problems with a minimum of conflict. In our work with families, we have found there are three things parents must do to be successful: (1) involve the adolescent in the problem-solving process, (2) learn how to control negative emotions, and (3) practice using specific problem-solving and negotiation skills.

Involving Adolescents in Decision Making

One of the most effective ways to protect your children is to have them participate in the process of setting the rules that govern their behavior. For example, adolescents can be included in making decisions about curfew hours, chores, routine responsibilities, sibling conflicts, house rules, and acceptable hairstyles and clothing. Group process can make it possible to resolve these family issues with a minimum of conflict. It also provides a legitimate way for adolescents to petition for new freedoms or special privileges, and it fosters their willingness to cooperate with the rules. This is better than letting teenagers achieve their goals by nagging, being sneaky, or using coercion. Perhaps most importantly, when adolescents are included in the decision-making process, they develop good problem-solving skills that can help them make the right choices when their parents or other responsible adults are not there.

Involving adolescents in making everyday family life decisions reduces conflict with parents in other ways. At some point during adolescence there is a shift of power that takes place in the minds of teenagers. During this stage, parents fall off the pedestal and teenagers climb on. When you begin to hear about your own shortcomings, it is a sign that the shift is occurring. Young children accept the fact that their parents are in charge; adolescents not only question this, they resent it. It is a quirk of nature that at 13 or 14 years of age teenagers assume they know everything about the world and that adults know very little. At this point the edicts passed down by parents are perceived as walls to push against, and discussions about rules start to heat up. Instead of having power struggles over who is in charge, it is better to redirect this energy by involving the adolescent in the decision-making process. Fortunately, when adolescents begin to question authority, they are also becoming more competent. Teenagers deserve more respect as their skills develop, and more of the rules that govern their behavior should be open for negotiation.

While group process is appropriate for most family issues, not everything is open for bargaining. For example, there is little room for compromise with the rule "No drinking or drug use while driving." But many other rules concerning less critical issues can be open for discussion. While each family may have a different perspective about which issues are negotiable, it is important to make decisions about this before the issues come up.

Some parents believe that children should not be involved in the process of setting rules or solving problems. They assume every problem has one correct solution and assert that it is their responsibility to make all of the decisions for the family. These parents dictate the rules, and everyone is expected to submit without question. In every situation, the authoritarian parent's will prevails. This approach may make life satisfying for the person in charge because time is not "wasted" on discussions and there are no compromises. While this strategy may work in the military, it is not recommended in families. The position taken by the authors emphasizes the need to involve family members in making decisions, establishing rules, and negotiating changes. To be effective, this must take place within an atmosphere of mutual respect.

Controlling Negative Emotions

It is difficult to negotiate differences and solve problems as a family if negative emotions take over. When problems are discussed, especially sensitive ones, people often become irritable (that is, testy or hostile), and this can quickly lead to conflict. If the discussion turns into a shouting match about past failures and injustices, any hope of resolving the issue is lost in the ensuing battle.

Parents must take charge of their own emotional reactions before they can help other family members stay calm. Some parents complain that their children yell and shout, say hateful things, have tantrums, and slam things around. When we ask parents to describe the circumstances surrounding these adolescent outbursts, we often find that the *parents* yell and shout, say hateful things, and have tantrums. The parents say they can't help it—their children drive them to it. But if you ask the adolescents why they behave as they do, guess whom they blame? If you guessed their parents, you are right (and so are they).

There are a few simple techniques that will help parents to control their own emotional responses. One such method is the old-fashioned routine of counting to 10 under your breath when you start to get angry. The worst thing you can do is to respond reflexively by saying the first thing that comes to mind. It is better to focus on your goal instead, which is to solve the problem. Venting anger on others is destructive, and it models inappropriate behavior for your children.

Many other techniques to keep family discussions from becoming heated are presented in this book. Using a structured approach for sensitive situations works well. The more sensitive the problem is, the more structured the approach should be to keep emotions from flaring up. We recommend holding a formal meeting, called a "family forum," to discuss difficult issues. The first section of this book presents detailed guidelines for setting up the family forum.

Problem-Solving Skills

Unfortunately, few of us have received any formal training in negotiation and problem-solving skills, which is one of the reasons we are sometimes overwhelmed by the challenges that confront us as parents of adolescents. These essential skills have not been made generally available to parents until recently. The principles presented here reflect work that has been carried out by psychologists during the last four decades.

Solving family problems is a challenge because they can be resolved in many different ways. Unlike math problems, there isn't *one* correct solution. Since each family is unique, the best solution to a particular problem must fit that family's set of values. It was mentioned in the preface that it is impossible to generate a convenient list of solutions to the problems faced by parents of adolescents. This book describes a set of procedures families can use to develop their own answers. The procedures are flexible, and they can be adapted to match each family's style and standards. A certain amount of trial and error is required, which can be frustrating. Through this process, however, you will be able to find solutions that work.

The problem-solving sequence has several steps: setting goals, presenting and receiving information, brainstorming solutions, evaluating solutions, making an agreement, and evaluating the outcomes. Our experience suggests that this problem-solving process works well for most families, but it takes practice to learn how to do it. The first section of this book describes each step in the problem-solving sequence in detail, and the homework exercises at the end of each chapter have been designed to help you develop the necessary skills. Working carefully through these exercises will improve your chances of success.

There are at least two approaches to problem solving that don't work. One is to pretend that problems don't exist. Don't bring up any sensitive issues, and there won't be any trouble. In these families (we call them the Avoiders), problems are not discussed, and, consequently, they are not solved either. The parents may notice, for example, that their adolescent sometimes comes home with red eyes, smelling faintly of marijuana. They ignore these warning signs, however, because if they allow themselves to see the problem, they may have to do something about it. For a long time there isn't any trouble, but little problems begin to pile up like snowflakes. Then, one day, the Avoiders realize they are surrounded by a snowdrift of problems, and they don't know where (or how) to begin working on them.

Another approach that doesn't resolve problems is to fight about them. In these families (we call them the Fighters), any attempt to manage a problem leads to conflict. Fighters give free rein to their feelings—they say exactly what they think, which makes *them* feel good, but it makes the problem worse. Instead of a family forum there is a family battlefield, and people are preoccupied with defending their positions rather than finding solutions. Problems also pile up in these families, but the snowdrift is periodically melted by the heat of conflict. In the cold war between skirmishes, the problems freeze together to form a wall of ice. When this happens, it is impossible to work on just one problem at a time.

It is dangerous to let family problems go untended. When an adolescent turns to drugs or fails in school, it may be the result of a series of unresolved issues. Over time, the accumulation of unplanned changes can turn the course of people's lives. Before you know it, the members of your family are no longer who you thought they were. It is up to parents to make active decisions about the course of growth and development they want for their family, and to provide the guidance that is necessary to achieve those goals.

Having a family is like caring for a very special garden. The goal is to help each plant thrive and reach its potential. It takes planning and constant care to be successful. If you let the weeds take over, the rest of the plants suffer. Each gardener has a slightly different style, but the gardens that flourish are the ones that receive the most planning and love.

Family Problems

Every family could improve the quality of life by making some changes, yet people rarely attempt to take the necessary steps during the early stages in the development of a problem. Our studies of families suggest that there is a good reason for this. Making changes in families means that *everyone* must be willing to change a little. The problem is that people often become angry or defensive when they are asked to change some aspect of their behavior, even when the request is justified. In effect, this punishes efforts to resolve problems when they are still small and manageable. Family members are trained to wait until problems become intolerable, which also makes them difficult to change.

Asking people to change does not mean you don't love them. It simply suggests that they are doing something that is creating problems for others. To keep the process in balance, however, people must take turns asking for and being asked to change, and this requires a high order of skill. The chapters that follow will teach you how to do this in a way that allows family members to feel good about each other and grow in positive directions.

Almost all family problems, large or small, are the outcome of a series of seemingly insignificant steps. These steps are made up of minute changes in the way family members relate to one another that are difficult to notice from one day to the next. Over time, however, these shifts can lead to dramatic outcomes. *Many of the battles between family members are caused by an accumulation of little things that need to be changed.*

The encouraging side of this picture is that families can interrupt destructive changes and initiate growth by altering the small steps in the sequence. This requires regular maintenance. We suggest having a family forum once each week to deal with issues while they are still manageable. Routinely working on little problems will help you to prevent big ones from developing. Weekly problem-solving sessions also enable you to chip away at the more serious problems that persist for months, or sometimes years.

Research Studies of Parent/Adolescent Relationships

Now for the good news. In a national survey, about 90% of 16-year-old boys and girls reported that they get along well with their mothers, and about 75% of the same sample said that they get along well with their fathers! This finding may be surprising because the media tend to portray the relationship between parents and adolescents as stormy and dominated by conflict. This stereotype, however, is not supported by research studies that have been carried out on normal families. These studies indicate that about one family in five reports difficult parent/child relationships. The majority of the adolescents said they are much more concerned about doing something that would lead to disapproval from their parents than disapproval from their peers.

Many parents feel that the disagreements they have with their adolescents reflect a rejection of their basic values. Arguments about hairstyles and manner of dress somehow have a special meaning for parents, who view this as a sign that their teenagers do not embrace the same beliefs as they do. In spite of how parents *feel* about this, the survey studies carried out during the last 10 years have shown that the vast majority of adolescents accept their parents' basic values. In one study surveyed, over 75% of the adolescents reported that they even accepted the discipline practices used by their parents. Parents do play an important role in determining the set of standards and values adopted by their children. Disagreements do not mean your adolescent is rejecting your values.

Even families fortunate enough to be part of the majority without serious problems have minor conflicts. Adolescent girls in normal families reported that on the average they have a minor conflict with their parents every 2 ½ days; the comparable rate for adolescent boys was one conflict every 4 days. Incidentally, about 75% of these conflicts were between adolescents and their mothers—it's fairly clear which parent is on the firing line. Most of the conflicts between mothers and daughters lasted about 15 minutes; conflicts with sons lasted about 6 minutes. Only about 50% of the adolescents surveyed reported participating in the process of setting house rules. We believe that negotiating house rules as a family would decrease the number of conflicts and increase the likelihood that adolescents will abide by them.

Even though these may be difficult times, take heart. Family problems can be managed constructively and fairly, and people can learn how to change. The principles outlined in this book will help you to plan your garden and make it flourish.

Introduction Homework Assignment

1. Introduce the idea of keeping a record of family disagreements and problems. Suggest that you would like to track how well your family manages such issues on a daily basis. This may include using the car, homework routines, or everyday household tasks. Explain that the long-term goal is to improve family relations by paying attention to what everyone wants and making the necessary changes.

2. Ask people to write notes about each issue that comes up during the coming week on the Tracking Sheet provided. The notes should be concise and clearly stated. (See the sample on the next page.) Post the Tracking Sheet on the refrigerator, a cabinet door, or some other convenient place so it is easy to find. Ask people to record every issue that concerns them by writing down the date, their name, and a brief statement of the issue. At this stage, don't try to identify the person(s) who are creating the issue because this will lead to conflict.

SAMPLE TRACKING SHEET

			Was the Issue Resolved?				
			Yes		Unclear		No
			1	2	3	4	5
Date	Name	Issue to Change					
12/3	Marion	Put cap on toothpaste after using it		2			
12/5	Erik	Use of car on Friday from 3 P.M. until curfew			3		
12/6	Jerry	Return hair dryer after borrowing it	1				
12/6	Jane	Trip to Portland: Leave Friday after school, return on Sunday at 9 P.M.					5

This record can be used in several ways. Sometimes simply listing an issue will prompt family members to change without having to discuss the problem. At other times, the record can serve as a list of issues that need to be considered during family meetings.

At the end of the week, ask someone to check with the people who listed issues on the Tracking Sheet. Have this person ask for ratings of whether the issue was resolved, using a 5-point scale: "1" means the issue was completely resolved, "3" indicates it is unclear whether it was resolved, and "5" suggests there was no resolution at all. Write these responses on the Tracking Sheet.

Post a new Tracking Sheet every week for the next several weeks. Create a family record book to save these Tracking Sheets and the other assignments to come.

TRACKING SHEET

			Was the Issue Resolved?		
			Yes	Unclear	No
			1 2	3	4 5
Date	Name	Issue to Change			

_____

_____

_____

_____

_____

_____

_____

_____

_____

_____

_____

SECTION I

Introduction

The first section of this book contains five chapters that provide step-by-step guidelines for solving problems and negotiating differences. Chapter 1 describes the communication skills necessary for effective problem solving. The process of brainstorming solutions is examined in Chapter 2, and methods for evaluating solutions are outlined in Chapter 3. The concept of discussing issues in a highly structured meeting, called a "family forum," is presented in Chapter 4. Some additional techniques for dealing with sensitive issues are offered in Chapter 5. The homework assignments in each chapter are designed to help family members practice new skills in problem-solving sessions and role-playing exercises.

Use this book as a workbook. As you read the chapters and follow the teaching dramas, write notes in the margin when you find a technique for regulating emotions or solving problems that might work for you. We hope this book will inspire you to think of additional ideas not covered here.

CHAPTER 1

Communication: The Key to Effective Problem Solving

There is a definite pattern to good communication: one person talks while the other person actively listens, and then the roles are reversed. In this way, conversations move forward and unfold. Each person responds to what has been said and contributes to the direction the conversation takes. It's like doing a dance in which both partners take turns leading and following. Couples who are good dancers are able to spin around the dance floor in perfect synchrony, responding to each other's subtle cues. In the same way, the balance between leading and following during communication can be improved by practicing the steps outlined in this chapter.

All of this sounds relatively simple—take turns and let the discussion unfold. This may be adequate for everyday conversations, but additional skills are required to talk about sensitive family issues. For that, you need techniques to control the negative emotions that often accompany conversations about delicate situations. It is difficult to stay calm when an issue is important or there is a difference of opinion, yet it is absolutely essential for a constructive exchange. Negative emotions disrupt the spirit of cooperation that is necessary for good communication and creative problem solving.

This book advocates using a structured approach to communicate about "hot" issues. You can tell an issue is hot if the temperature rises slightly whenever the topic comes up. The guidelines for communicating about family issues are like the routines for an intricate dance. Instead of leading and following, the mutual exchange involves presenting and receiving information. It is possible to have cool discussions about hot topics if you use a structured approach.

To resolve complicated family problems, people have to be open to new ideas. If "the same old way" hasn't been working, it's time to try something new. You may find that the techniques presented in this chapter feel awkward at first. This is actually a good sign, because it means you are taking the risk of learning a new skill. Dancers always feel a little clumsy when they learn a new routine. With practice, however, your communication skills will improve, and you will be able to add some of your own moves to the steps outlined here.

The next section outlines some basic skills for discussing neutral issues, such as events of the day. The focus is on being a good listener. The procedures for communicating about family problems build on these skills by adding several other components to control negative emotions.

The Importance of Being a Good Listener

When the communication process in families breaks down, it is difficult to have a rational discussion about even neutral topics. Conversations that start out well may end in tears or anger, and nobody can figure out what happened. Sometimes it is a simple case of poor listening skills.

Good listeners clearly convey that they are interested in what other people are saying. One of the basic elements is to pay attention when someone else is talking, but there are other elements as well. The following are some tips for being a good listener.

Guidelines for Good Listening

1. **When the other person is speaking, visualize the story in your mind.** For example, if your son is on the football team and he is explaining one of the plays, picture how it would look on the field. You will need to ask questions to complete the picture. Asking questions is also a good way to let the speaker know that you are interested in the topic.

2. **Try to learn something from the speaker.** If your daughter is studying chemistry, for example, ask her to teach you about the subject. Listen carefully, and don't be afraid to admit that you don't understand everything. Assume the role of the student, and let the adolescent be the teacher.

3. **Stay focused on what the other person is telling you.** Don't use the conversation as an opportunity to tell one of your favorite stories about the time when you . . .

4. **Ask questions that move the conversation along.** The quality of the questions asked by the listener affects the information given by the presenter. You can help each other become better storytellers by asking questions about interesting details.

5. **Try to match the other person's emotional state unless it is hostile.** If the speaker is enthusiastic and your response is lackluster, that person will feel rejected. If you try to humor someone who is feeling sad without reflecting on his or her melancholy mood, that person will feel misunderstood. A good listener knows how to be empathetic.

6. **Do not give advice unless you are asked to.** Simply concentrate on what the other person is saying, and show that you are interested.

7. **Try to understand the other person's perspective.** Think about how you would feel if you were in the other person's shoes. If you disagree or disapprove, don't show it.

8. **Think before you respond.** An excellent way to practice this is to count silently to 10 with a calm expression on your face before speaking. It is easy to put your foot in your mouth if you

respond reflexively, and the other person will often fill in the blank if you create an opportunity for him or her to do so.

The following is a teaching drama that illustrates how these guidelines work.

Act I: Angela Gets the Lead

The Scene. Angela's father has just arrived to pick her up from a ballet lesson.

Angela is 15, and she has taken ballet lessons for several years. Her teacher has repeatedly commented on her exceptional progress. Her father, however, has never been interested in ballet.

Angela: (She jumps in the car, throws her stuff in the backseat, and leans over to kiss her father on the cheek.) Hi, Dad. Guess what?

Dad: (He smiles in response to her obvious good mood.) You won the lottery!

Angela: No, but you're on the right track. I got the lead in *Romeo and Juliet!*

Dad: (He smiles briefly and tries to sound excited, but he is concerned about how this new turn of events will affect Angela's performance in school. His voice betrays his reservation as he replies.) Well, that's great, but won't that interfere with your schoolwork?

Angela: (Her disappointment is obvious. She has worked long and hard to earn a chance to play a leading role, and her own father doesn't seem to care. She slumps down in her seat as she thinks about all the times her father has missed her ballet recitals.) I think I can manage.

Dad: What's the matter with you? Are you in another one of your moods? (Angela just stares out the window without answering.)

Commentary

What could Angela's father have done to convey that he was pleased with his daughter's success? Think of three or four responses that would have been more tactful before you read the replay of this scene. This time Dad is a better listener.

Angela: I got the lead in *Romeo and Juliet!*

Dad: (He makes a genuine and quite successful attempt to match her enthusiasm.) You did? That's terrific! You must be very excited.

Angela: Oh, I am! You *know* how hard I worked for this, and I was afraid Nancy would get the part.

Dad: (He's happy for her, but he realizes there will be daily rehearsals and her grades might slip. However, he knows that he can discuss this with her later. Now it is Angela's time to shine and feel good about her accomplishment. He asks her to tell him more about the ballet and her role in it.) Where will it be performed, at the school?

Angela: (Her face lights up.) No, it's going to be at the Community Center for the Performing Arts! They have a full-size stage! And we're going to do several of our rehearsals there so we can get used to the stage, the spotlights, and everything!

Dad: He turns and smiles. Angela's excitement seems boundless.) I don't know much about ballet, as you know. Tell me about *Romeo and Juliet.*

Angela is pleased that her father seems interested, and she tells him the story of Romeo and Juliet. Then she goes on to describe how her group is going to do the performance. Her enthusiasm is infectious, and by the time they reach home they are both in a great mood and Angela feels close to her father.

Commentary

It should be easy to listen to someone else talk about the happy events in their lives, but sometimes we become so involved in our own concerns that we forget to notice anyone else. It is more difficult, however, to be a good listener when someone is talking about a topic that is worrisome. This is illustrated in the following teaching drama in which a conversation takes place between an adolescent girl and her mother.

Act I: Bumper Bashing

The Scene. Seventeen-year-old Nancy is working in the garden with her mother. This has always been a pleasant activity for both of them. Nancy's mother had given her a tomato plant when she was six years old. That plant had produced an abundance of large and delicious tomatoes, and Nancy and her mother have enjoyed growing things together ever since. Many of their best conversations have taken place while tending the garden. The discussion begins as Nancy tells her mother about something that happened to her best friend, Harriet.

Nancy: Boy, Harriet's really going to get in trouble if her mother finds out about the car.

Mom: Really? What happened to the car?

Nancy: Oh, nothing. I guess I shouldn't tell you, anyway. You'd only tell her mother, and then Harriet would get mad at me.

Mom: Oh. (Although she's dying to hear more, she decides not to take the bait right away. As she digs around a particularly sturdy weed, she counts slowly to herself to 10.) So, Harriet had a problem with the car?

Nancy: Yeah! I'm so glad I'm not her.

Mom: It must have been pretty bad.

Nancy: Well, I'll tell you what happened if you promise not to tell her mother.

Mom: (This is a hard decision for Mom to make. What if Harriet did something really terrible? Wouldn't she be duty-bound to tell Harriet's mother? But she also realizes that there is no way to help if she doesn't know what happened. Nancy obviously wants to talk about it. Mom decides to agree to keep the secret.) OK, I promise not to tell. What happened?

Nancy: We were downtown and Harriet was trying to parallel park the car so we could go shopping, but she was having trouble getting the car close enough to the curb. She went back and forth trying to park the car at least a dozen times, like a sideways yo-yo.

Mom: (She bursts out laughing.) I can just imagine that!

Nancy: Everything was all right until her foot slipped off the clutch, and we bashed into the car in front of us.

Mom: Oh, no! Was anybody hurt?

Nancy: No, but the car was.

Mom: Is she a bad driver, or is it just parallel parking that's the problem?

Nancy: Neither. It was something else.

Mom: What was that?

Nancy: (She looks uncomfortable, as though she just let something slip that she shouldn't have.) Oh, nothing. The part I was going to tell you about is that she hasn't told her mother about the car.

Mom: She hasn't! How come? (Nancy's secretiveness upsets Mom. She is worried that alcohol or marijuana might have been involved in the accident, but she decides not to pursue that right now.)

Nancy: Because if she does, she may never get to use the car again.

Commentary

This is a critical point in the conversation. There are several ways Mom could respond that would end the conversation or guarantee that Nancy will never tell her anything important again (think of five such responses before reading the list that follows).

1. She could express her disapproval of Harriet's irresponsible behavior.
2. She could give a lecture regarding her concerns about Nancy's driving.
3. She could tell Nancy never to ride with Harriet again.
4. She could insist that Nancy tell her about the missing information.
5. She could break her promise and tell Harriet's mother about the incident.

Any one of these responses would probably stop the flow of information. Even though Mom disapproves, she can still do a good job of listening if she tries to understand the story from Harriet's perspective. She can always bring up the topic some other time and probe for more information then. If she does this now, after Nancy has initiated the conversation, she will be punishing Nancy for confiding in her. Let's see how the conversation unfolds.

Mom: I'll bet Harriet is really upset about this.

Nancy: She is. The accident happened a couple of days ago, and Harriet is worried sick about it. She's afraid her mom will notice the dent in the bumper and know she did it.

Mom: Is the car badly damaged?

Nancy: Not really. (They work together silently for a while.) Actually, I think she should tell her mom and get it over with. Otherwise, she'll be a nervous wreck forever.

Mom: (She is really tempted to give advice at this point, but she decides to be sympathetic.) What a terrible position to be in.

Nancy: Yeah. What would you do if I did that?

Mom: (This comment makes Mom wonder if she should check the bumpers on *their* car, but she laughs in a friendly way.) Do you have something you want to tell me?

Nancy: No, I was just wondering. What would you do?

Mom: Hmmm. (She thinks for a minute.) What do you think I should do?

Nancy: (She sighs.) Oh, Mom. You always answer questions with more questions.

Mom: (laughs) I just do that when I need more time to think.

Commentary

This conversation stayed out of the danger zone. What were the things both of them did that helped to make it a pleasant exchange? How do you think Mom can keep the lines of communication open and deal with her concerns at the same time? Just for practice, write your thoughts on a piece of paper.

The two teaching dramas presented so far illustrate how to communicate about issues that aren't too sensitive. The discussion in the first drama was about a relatively cool issue. In the second drama, the issue was a little warmer because there was the added element of parental concern. It is more difficult to communicate about personal problems, however, because they are usually accompanied by strong feelings and the discussion can heat up quickly. The next section of this chapter describes how to deal with sensitive issues (additional information is provided in Chapter 5).

Communicating about Family Problems

It is best to use a structured approach when you are discussing difficult problems. This prevents negative emotions from interrupting the communication process. If you want to *solve* problems as a family, not just talk about them, you must avoid getting swept away by feelings such as anger, anxiety, contempt, and despair. Such negative emotions tend to elicit the same negative reactions from others, and rational thinking falls by the wayside.

Presenting Information

In the first stage of problem solving someone must present the issue to another person or to the whole family. This person is called the "Presenter." The way in which an issue is presented has a powerful effect on how it is received, because it sets the tone for the discussion that follows. Here are some guidelines for presenting issues that will help to maintain a positive atmosphere for the discussion.

Guidelines for Presenters

1. **Make the statement short.** Pare the words down to an absolute minimum. This is not the time for lectures. You can get on your soapbox some other time.
2. **Be pleasant.** Make your presentation as palatable as possible by using neutral words, an agreeable tone of voice, and appropriate facial expressions and general body posture. Do not use loaded words, or hostile tones and gestures.
3. **Say something nice about the other person.** It's important to be sincere when you do this. Think about the things you like about the person when you are not mad. Write them down so

you will remember them as you talk. If you can't say something nice, then try one of the next suggestions.

4. **Show that you understand the other person's point of view.** Parents should try to remember what it was like when they were adolescents. Teenagers should also try to imagine how they would feel if they were the parents in a given situation.

5. **Recognize your part in the problem.** Take some of the blame on your shoulders. The "victim" of an issue often plays a significant role in the development and/or maintenance of the problem.

6. **Use humor if you can do it without adding sarcasm.** Humor means laughing at yourself or the circumstances, not at the other person. When humor is used skillfully, it can turn a tense situation into a pleasant and creative family discussion.

7. **Think of the future.** State what you want today, tomorrow, or next week. Avoid talking about the past unless it is used as an example of something good. Talking about past mistakes and problems leads to defensive reactions.

8. **State the behavior you want.** If you tell someone what you *don't* want, you still haven't identified the behavior you would like to see more of.

9. **State your goal as simply and specifically as possible.** This often means thinking about what you want ideally. You may not achieve perfection, but you can try for it. Emphasize long-term goals.

The Presenter usually sees the problem from a limited point of view, and other family members may have different opinions. The goal of the presenting and receiving process is for everyone to share perspectives on the issue. Convey interest in each other's point of view, and make sure everyone is involved. Avoid taking sides or judging who is right and who is wrong because this will stop the exchange.

As information is presented and received, you may find that the definition of the problem shifts like sand dunes in the wind. Believe it or not, this is a good sign. The way the family views the problem *should* expand and change if everyone's position on the subject is considered.

Receiving Information

The person who is being asked to change is called the "Receiver." It is this person's job to pay attention to the Presenter's message. This requires focusing on exactly what the *other* person is saying, listening for key words in the message, and restating in your own words what the Presenter has said. Here are some guidelines for receiving information about an issue.

Guidelines for Receivers

1. **Use active listening skills.** To show that you understand what has been said, paraphrase the Presenter's statement. Paraphrasing means to briefly recap the other person's statement.
2. **Don't add your own thoughts or feelings to the message.** You will have a chance to do this later.
3. **Don't be defensive.** When someone asks you to change, don't make excuses, even if you feel justified in doing so.
4. **Maintain a neutral position.** You don't have to agree or disagree with the Presenter's point of view. Simply listen and understand.
5. **Don't criticize the Presenter.** It may be tempting to attack the Presenter, particularly if you have been criticized, but this is counterproductive. If there are things about the Presenter's behavior you think need to be changed, take this up at another time.
6. **Listen for the positive side of the message.** Accept the message at face value. Don't read negative intentions into the statement. Try to focus on the constructive aspects of the Presenter's suggestions.
7. **Be pleasant.** Maintain a calm demeanor and tone of voice, and use neutral words.
8. **Show respect for the Presenter.** Treat the Presenter with the same courtesy you would give a stranger or a good friend

whom you don't want to offend. We call this the "Stranger Rule."

9. **Remember: The Presenter is someone you care about, not an enemy.** Your goal is to learn how to get along peacefully, not to generate conflict.

Checking Signals

After the Presenter introduces the issue and the Receiver has paraphrased it, the Presenter should confirm whether or not the information has been accurately received. If not, then the Presenter must restate the problem. When the message has been correctly received, the Presenter and Receiver change roles. This is the next stage in the communication process.

Let's look at several teaching dramas that illustrate the "wrong way" and "right way" to present and receive information during the first and second stages of communication.

Act I: A Little Privacy, Please

The Scene. Michelle is 13, and she shares her bedroom with her 8-year-old sister, Kara. Michelle would love to have her friends come home with her after school, but Kara is always there. Her specific goal is to be able to go into her bedroom with her friends without Kara hanging around.

The first time Michelle states her issue, she violates several of the guidelines for Presenters. She feels angry and hopeless, and that is the message she sends. Notice the effect this has on the communication process.

Michelle: Kara has ruined my social life. Nobody wants to come to my house anymore because Kara is always in the way. (whining) I don't think it's fair that I can't ever keep her out of my room.

Mom: (sounding a little irritated) You have the sensitivity of an elephant. Look at how you just made your sister cry.

She doesn't ruin your social life! You do, with your rotten attitude!

Michelle: You always take her side! Why can't I have my friends over without her bugging us?

Mom: You're just selfish.

Commentary

Notice how Michelle's feelings interfere with her goal of having a little privacy. If she could control those feelings, she would make more progress toward resolving the issue. Let's look at a better approach.

Michelle: (She smiles sweetly at her little sister and begins.) You know, Kara, I can understand that you like to hang out with us when my friends come over. I guess I might feel that way, too, if I were you. (humorously) After all, we are so charming. (Everyone laughs at this, even Kara.)

Mom: Who should be the person to "receive" your message, Michelle? Kara?

Michelle: I guess so.

Mom: So, Kara, that means you have to repeat what Michelle just said.

Kara: (whining) Why?

Michelle frowns because she thinks her little sister will get what she wants, which is what usually happens. Mom quickly intervenes because she wants to help the girls develop better communication skills. Michelle did a good job of getting started, and Mom would like the discussion to continue following a constructive course.

Mom: Kara, we are practicing communication skills, and people show they are listening by repeating what the other person just said.

Kara: That's dumb.

Mom: Kara, that comment is not appropriate. If you don't want to help us solve this problem, you can leave the room and someone else will speak for you.

Kara: No, I'll do it myself. Michelle can't understand why I want to be in my room when her friends are there.

Mom: Michelle, is that right?

Michelle: I guess so. (She smiles in a gentle, teasing manner.) But she forgot the charming part.

Mom: (Smiling at this attempt at humor, she is pleased with the way Michelle is handling the situation.) Is there anything else you would like to say?

Michelle: Yes. I wanted to say that us old ladies have things to talk about that should not be heard by younger sisters. So I'd appreciate it, Kara, if we could have a little privacy. That means time alone in the bedroom with the door closed, please.

Kara: You mean you want me to stay out of the room when you have your girlfriends around?

Michelle: Yes.

Mom: (She intervenes before something goes wrong.) That was very well done by both of you.

Commentary

Michelle's positive attitude in the second presentation made a big difference. A little understanding, some humor, and a clear statement of what she wanted made Michelle's approach much more effective. Several pitfalls were avoided in that scene. Make a list of some of the ways this discussion could have taken a wrong turn. Can you think of some other ways that Michelle's presentation could have been improved?

The next teaching drama involves an issue that is a concern for many parents.

Act I: We Wish You Were College Bound

The Scene. Kobin is a senior in high school, and his parents are afraid that he may not go to college. He's a straight-A student, but he is not bringing home college catalogs, preparing for the SAT, or making plans like other college-bound seniors. The scene begins as Dad presents the issue. (When two parents are concerned about the same issue, one parent should do the presenting while the other one simply listens.)

Dad: Kobin, your mother and I have agreed that I should be the Presenter for this issue.

Kobin: Sure, Dad. What's the problem?

Dad: As you know, we think a college education is important, and we are worried that you aren't making the necessary preparations.

Kobin: OK. You guys are afraid I'll *never* go to college, even though you think it's important.

Commentary

This presentation does not have any blatant errors, but there are a few things missing. What are they?

If you noticed that Dad didn't say something positive or that he didn't make an effort to assume some responsibility for the situation, you are right on track. Did you also notice that Kobin was doing a little mind reading when he added the word "never"? Here's a better start.

Dad: I'm not sure how to present this issue without making you feel defensive, so please bear with me if I'm a little clumsy.

Kobin: (laughing in a friendly way) Oh, no—this must be heavy if you're afraid of being awkward.

Dad: (chuckles nervously) Well, it's about college. You are such a good student, and your mother and I are both very proud of you. The issue is that we are concerned you may not be planning to go to college this year, and we want you to go.

Kobin: I guess it is a heavy issue. You're proud of me, but you're afraid I'm not planning to go to college next year. And you want me to go. Is that right?

Dad: Yes, that's right!

Commentary

It's all right to admit that you are anxious as you present an issue. Sometimes that even helps to make the Receiver more open to your message. The key is to be as positive as possible and to clearly state what you want. Let's look at one more example of the first stage of presenting and receiving before we move on to the second stage in the communication process.

Act I: Nobody Comes to Our House

The Scene. Rebecca is 15. Her mother is concerned because Rebecca never brings her friends home. Mom is worried that Rebecca's friends may be disreputable and that she is ashamed to introduce them to her family. Mom has decided not to allow Rebecca out at night unless Mom meets the friends she's going with.

Mom: Rebecca, from now on you cannot go out in the evening unless I have met the kids you're going with. That means you'd better start bringing your friends home more often.

Rebecca: (This takes Rebecca by surprise. She grimaces and starts whining loudly.) Mom, that's really stupid. Nobody does that these days. You're just being old-fashioned.

Mom: (firmly) Old-fashioned or not, that's how it's going to be.

Rebecca: I don't want to bring my friends home because everyone runs around here arguing and yelling, and it's embarrassing.

Mom: But *you're* the one who starts the yelling.

Commentary

This conversation immediately turned into an argument. Mom's presentation was relatively straightforward, but her first statement was a demand, and she did nothing to soften it. Mom also stated *her* solution to the problem as part of the presentation. A good presentation does not include threats about impending consequences. The goal is to describe the problem in neutral terms and to work together to *negotiate* a solution. Mom's job here was to begin the discussion in a positive way and then simply state that she wants Rebecca to bring her friends home more often. Let's look at a more effective approach.

> **Mom:** I feel like I'm missing out on an important part of your life by not knowing your friends. I would really like to meet them. I know the last time you brought someone home we were having a family crisis, but that won't happen every time. Could you invite your friends over more often?
>
> **Rebecca:** You want me to have my friends over here more often, even though last time we had a big fight.
>
> **Mom:** Yes, that's right.

Commentary

Mom followed the guidelines by recognizing her contribution to the problem (the family crisis), and then she stated what she wanted. Mom's presentation was straightforward and pleasant. Rebecca paraphrased the message but added a little emotional charge by referring to the "big fight." Mom wisely agreed instead of reacting defensively. Now they are ready to move the conversation forward.

The next stage in the communication process involves having the Presenter and Receiver change roles.

Changing Roles—The Receiver Presents

The Receiver will cooperate with the communication process more readily if there is an opportunity to present his or her side of the story. After the original message has been presented and received, the roles are reversed. Now the Receiver presents another perspective while the original Presenter assumes the role of Receiver.

It is a good idea to take a short break before continuing on to this next stage to give everyone a chance to change roles. The new Presenter must now express in a few words how he or she sees the problem. It is important to become *neither aggressive nor defensive* in making this presentation. Think of one piece of information that is particularly important from your perspective and introduce it in a positive light. All of the guidelines described earlier for the Presenter also apply to the "new" Presenter. Review these guidelines before reading the continuation of our earlier teaching dramas.

Act II: Hanging Out with Big Sister

The Scene. Before the family took a short break, Mom asked Michelle for permission to "coach" Kara. Michelle hesitated at first because she thought this would give Kara an unfair edge, but Mom pointed out that since Michelle was older and wiser, Kara was at a disadvantage. Michelle finally agreed. Now the conversation continues.

Kara: OK. Now it's my turn. Michelle, I just want to hang out when you have your friends around.

Mom: Wait a minute. Remember to say something nice to Michelle at the beginning.

Kara: Oh, that's right. Ummm. (She bites her lip as she tries to remember what she and her mom had practiced.) Michelle, I think you and your friends are really neat. How can I ever learn to be cool if I don't have a chance to hang out with you?

Michelle: Oh, gag me with a rag. Things are getting a little thick around here.

Mom: Michelle, I want you to be nice! Your job is to paraphrase.

Michelle: I'm sorry. Recognizing how rad me and my friends are, you want to bask in our glory.

Kara: Mom, I didn't say that.

Mom: Michelle, just paraphrase. Please!

Michelle: Sorry. You want to hang out with us so you can be trendy like us.

Kara: Yeah!

Mom: OK, that's good.

Commentary

Sometimes it helps to have a mediator, which is the role Mom assumed in this last scene. Can you think of some other ways Kara could have presented the issue to Michelle?

Act II: College Can Wait

The Scene. The college dilemma continues to unfold as Kobin now takes the role of Presenter and his father receives.

Kobin: I appreciate your concern about me going to college. I agree that it's really important. And I do plan to go eventually. But I want to take a year off before I sign up for another four years of studying.

Dad: But if you don't go right away, you may get sidetracked.

Kobin: No fair, Dad. You're not supposed to move on. You're supposed to paraphrase what I'm saying.

Dad: Sorry, son. You said that you understand how important college is, but you need a break before you hit the books for another four years. Is that better?

Kobin: (smiling at how well this is going) Yeah. (gently teasing) *Good job,* Dad.

Commentary

Notice that the missing piece of information finally emerged during stage two in the communication process. Dad and Mom now understand their son's college plans, even though they may not approve.

Act II: I'll Bring My Friends Home If . . .

The Scene. Rebecca is now the Presenter as her mother listens to her concerns about bringing friends home.

Rebecca: This is going to be hard to explain without making you mad. You're a great mother and all that stuff, but whenever I have a friend over, somebody's always raising a fuss, and that's embarrassing. How would you like it if you brought someone home and everyone started yelling?

Mom: Not very much, I suppose.

Rebecca: Well, that's the problem. Couldn't we have an agreement that people won't have arguments while my friends are here?

Mom: Wait a minute! I need to catch up on my paraphrasing. It seems like someone always raises a fuss when your friends visit, and you would like us to agree not to have verbal boxing matches when your friends are here. Is that right?

Rebecca: Yes, Mom. That is exactly what I'm trying to say.

Commentary

This exchange was well managed by Rebecca and her mother. Now it is clearly understood that Rebecca would feel more comfortable about bringing friends home if family members would agree not to have arguments while her friends are visiting.

Once your family learns how to make careful presentations and use active listening skills, you will be able to resolve *relatively simple* problems with little effort. The next drama illustrates how this might work.

Act I: Trouble at the Dinner Table

The Scene. The cast of characters in this next drama were introduced in Part 1 of this mini-series. Ida and her 16-year-old daughter, Carole, live alone together. The following conversation takes place as they discuss Carole's habit of coming home late for dinner.

Ida: Carole, the night before last you came home an hour late for dinner, and last night you didn't get home until 8:30. I was worried about you and didn't know what to do.

Carole: (looking up from her plate with a scowl on her face) I wasn't an hour late the night before last—it might have been 30 minutes at the most. You are always exaggerating. And I told you I was going to be late last night, but you just forgot. What's new about that?

Commentary

Let's start out with what was right about the Presenter's message. It was short.

Now for what was wrong. There was a description of Carole's behavior (you were late) and a feeling statement (I was worried). These seem reasonable enough. The problem is that both statements led directly to Carole defending herself and attacking Ida. Ida's descriptive statement was actually criticism, and her feeling statement was a guilt message.

How could Ida improve her presentation? Make a list of your own suggestions before moving on to a retake of the same scene.

Ida: (Ida and Carole are having a pleasant conversation during dinner about the events of the day.) I enjoy our dinners together. It's the one relaxing time of the day when we can share what's happening.

Carole: I really like nights like tonight when we aren't hassling each other.

Ida: Me, too! How can we make this happen more often?

Carole: Just by being nicer to each other.

Ida: I agree. And by making sure that we sit down together for dinner. (She takes a bite of her salad and chews it thoughtfully. They are comfortably silent for a while.) What if we set a regular time for dinner and make it kind of sacred? I think we should both make a special effort to be here and be pleasant.

Carole: So you want to set a regular time for dinner, and try to be pleasant. That sounds good to me.

Ida: Yes, that's it exactly!

Carole: But you know, there's one small problem. I have drama practice on Tuesday and Thursday afternoons, and I don't get out until almost six. That's why I'm late for dinner.

Ida: Hmmm. Drama on Tuesday and Thursday until six. What's a better dinnertime for you?

Carole: How about 6:30? I think I could be home by then.

Ida: OK, 6:30 is a good time. I'll make sure I have dinner ready by then. If you are going to be later than that, could you call me?

Carole: Sure, I guess so.

Ida: Then we'll have dinner at 6:30, and we'll both be pleasant. And if you're going to be late, you'll call. Right?

Carole: OK, let's give it a try.

Commentary

There were several things that turned this discussion into a mini-problem-solving session. In fact, it went so well that they were able to resolve the entire issue in approximately two minutes. Read the scene again and write down everything you thought contributed to the successful outcome before you look at the following list.

The Elements of Success

1. The stage was set for success because Carole and Ida were already in good moods. Ida's statement about relaxing and sharing during dinnertime was a positive way to introduce the subject.
2. Carole's comment about not hassling could have sidetracked the discussion into an argument about who starts the hassles; but Ida deftly kept things on track by agreeing with Carole.
3. Ida's first goal statement was the question "How can we make this happen more often?" That elicited *positive input* from Carole. Notice that it was future oriented.
4. Carole, who was the Receiver, was paraphrasing Ida's statements. She was neither attacking nor reacting defensively, and most of her input contributed to the forward movement of the discussion. Ida agreed and moved the discussion one step fur-

ther by clearly stating what she wanted (having dinner to-gether).

5. It may seem silly to mention that Ida paused while she chewed her salad, but when you have conversations it is a good idea to regularly provide each other with well-timed opportunities to speak. Sometimes we get so focused on achieving goals that we do too much talking. Get in the habit of pausing during your interactions to give others a chance to talk.

6. Ida's next few lines ("What if we set a time . . . ?") were again suggestions phrased as questions that involved both of them in the discussion because she used the words "we" and "both."

7. Carole indicated that she liked the idea, and then she brought up the problem of drama practice on Tuesday and Thursday after-noons. This was something Ida had not considered before. It's surprising how many times problems come up because parents and adolescents forget to communicate about these small details.

8. Ida finally solved the drama practice dilemma by suggesting they have dinner at a different time, and the idea was readily accepted. Ida then added one more little detail—Carole should call if she is going to be late. Ida also summed up the agreement: Dinnertime is 6:30, both of them will be pleasant, and Carole will call if she is going to be late.

When you are communicating about an issue, don't try to agree on what to do about it unless things happen to fall into place quickly, as in this last example. During the stages of presenting and receiving, you simply want to exchange information about the problem.

Key Ideas in This Chapter

1. Communication involves presenting and receiving information.
2. Good listening skills improve the communication process.
3. A structured approach is recommended for discussing sensitive family issues.
4. During stage one of the communication process, the Presenter states the issue, and the Receiver paraphrases what is said.
5. During stage two, the Presenter and Receiver change roles.

6. The function of a mediator is to keep the discussion moving in a positive direction.

Chapter One Homework Assignment

1. Without explaining that you are doing something new, practice using active listening skills with your adolescent by following the guidelines presented in this chapter.

2. Keep track of the way family members communicate with one another. Record in a notebook your observations about what people are doing right and what they are doing wrong. Make an effort to look for an equal number of "rights" and "wrongs."

3. Introduce the idea of practicing communication skills to your family. Describe the process of presenting and receiving by showing the guidelines to the family. Select two or three of the situations provided in the practice exercises that follow, and practice presenting and receiving information about them. Take turns playing different roles; the parents should sometimes play the role of the teenager and vice versa. This exercise can be a lot of fun if you give it a good introduction.

Practice Exercises

1. Will wants to have a friend overnight, but the last time he was allowed to do this he played his stereo late into the night. Then he and his dad got into a terrible fight, and they ended up yelling and shouting and slamming things around.
2. Dad does not want telephone calls to be made to or from the house after 9 P.M. He goes to bed early and phone calls wake him up. Dad believes this is probably true in other families as well.
3. Mom wants the children to have decent table manners. She had a friend over for dinner recently and was embarrassed by her children's rudeness.
4. Seventeen-year-old Margaret wants to drive four of her friends to the football game in the family car. The last time she had the

car, she returned it with no gas in the tank and she didn't park it in the garage where it belonged. In addition, her parents are worried that their insurance premiums will increase dramatically if Margaret has an accident.

5. Dad would like to improve the content of the conversations at dinnertime. He feels that the current discussions focus on trivial events rather than addressing topics that would be more interesting and thought provoking.

6. Tim would like his mother to stop nagging him when his friends are around. Every time he brings someone home, she seems to find an opportunity to describe all of the things he has done lately that upset her.

7. Mom has a stressful job, and she would like to have 20 minutes of absolute peace when she comes home after work. When she walks in the door it seems as though everyone wants to talk to her at once, and it's usually about problems. Instead of wanting to come home to her family, she dreads it because she feels bombarded with problems to solve.

8. Eighteen-year-old Sally wants to go shopping in a city 200 miles away because she can get the latest fashions there. She has already earned the money to pay for the clothes.

9. Miles wants his parents to let his best friend move in with them because his friend's parents have moved away and the boy has no place to live while he finishes his senior year at high school.

10. Jessyca's mother has just remarried, and her new husband has brought Carl, his seven-year-old boy, into the family. Jessyca thinks Carl is a brat, and she wants him to leave her and her things alone.

11. Scot plays the saxophone; but every time he tries to practice, his little brother starts to cry. Scot wants to be able to practice the saxophone without feeling guilty about it.

12. Mom wants Jan to practice the piano for one hour each day. Jan begged her mom to get a piano, and she promised to take lessons and practice faithfully. Now, the only time Jan practices is when Mom nags her about it.

13. Shannon wants to get her own car. She has saved some money for the car, but she doesn't have enough to pay for insurance. She considers the mandatory insurance rule to be ridiculous and thinks it is none of her parents' business anyway.

14. Tara wants her brother and his friends to be more polite to her. They don't like having Tara around because she's a girl and she's younger than they are. Tara thinks this is unfair, and she is tired of being teased and hassled in her own home.

Guidelines for Good Listening

1. When the other person is speaking, visualize the story in your mind.
2. Try to learn something from the speaker.
3. Stay focused on what the other person is telling you.
4. Ask questions that move the conversation along.
5. Try to match the other person's emotional state, unless it is hostile.
6. Do not give advice unless you are asked to.
7. Try to understand the other person's perspective.
8. Think before you respond.

Guidelines for Presenters

1. Make the statement short.
2. Be pleasant.
3. Say something nice about the other person.
4. Show that you understand the other person's point of view.
5. Recognize your part in the problem.
6. Use humor if you can do it without adding sarcasm.
7. Think of the future.
8. State the behavior you want.
9. State your goal as simply and specifically as possible.

Guidelines for Receivers

1. Use active listening skills.
2. Don't add your own thoughts or feelings to the message.
3. Don't be defensive.
4. Maintain a neutral position.
5. Don't criticize the Presenter.
6. Listen for the positive side of the message.
7. Be pleasant.
8. Show respect for the Presenter.
9. Remember that the Presenter is someone you care about, not an enemy.

CHAPTER 2

Brainstorming Solutions

This chapter describes how to work together as a family to develop solutions to problems. Learning how to communicate about issues is an important first step, but it is also necessary to come up with a plan of action to improve the situation. A technique that works well is to have everyone participate in generating a list of possible solutions to the problem. This process is called "brainstorming." During the brainstorming stage, family members are encouraged to think creatively about how to solve the problem. This produces a rich supply of options that represent everyone's perspective on an issue. Each idea is taken seriously and is written down on a list. The suggestions are not evaluated until later, because that stops the flow of ideas.

It is important to create a relaxed atmosphere for brainstorming. The goal is to make everyone feel comfortable about sharing ideas with the group. Criticism makes people reluctant to contribute to the discussion, so disparaging remarks are not allowed. Brainstorming can be an enjoyable event if you approach it with a positive attitude. You may even have some good laughs together if you use a little humor.

Brainstorming sessions are more productive if specific rules are observed. As in the other aspects of problem solving, these rules are designed to encourage cooperation among family members and to prevent negative emotions from interfering with the brainstorming process.

Guidelines for Brainstorming

1. **Involve everyone in the process.** The goal is to make sure that each person offers about the same number of suggestions. Some families have at least one high-rate idea person, and it may be necessary to take steps to prevent someone from dominating the discussion. There may also be quiet or shy members of the family who need some encouragement.

2. **Take turns.**

3. **Come up with at least five possible solutions.**

4. **Encourage creativity.** At this point, the sky is the limit.

5. **Do not evaluate ideas.** The purpose of brainstorming is to generate as many options as possible, and endorsing or rejecting suggestions will stop the stream of ideas.

6. **Record *every* suggestion, even if it seems ridiculous.** It can be helpful to suggest an idea that is a little outrageous every now and then. This makes everyone feel less self-conscious, and the idea may have some merit.

7. **Do not allow criticism or hostility.** This means don't make faces, use malicious gestures, or permit comments like, "Don't be silly," or, "That's stupid." Criticism interrupts the creative process, and personal attacks make people angry.

8. **Be neutral about the ideas you dislike.** Make brief comments such as, "All right," "That's an idea," or, "Let's write that down."

9. **Use humor occasionally.** Be playful and light, but don't do it at someone else's expense. Some of the best ideas grow out of laughter.

10. **Write down rule violations.** Write each person's name on a piece of paper and record rule infractions. After any one per-

son has three violations, either stop the session or have that person leave the discussion for five minutes.

11. **If the discussion becomes heated, take a five-minute break or postpone the session until later.** Negative emotions can quickly flare up during discussions about sensitive family issues. A little cooling-off time can help you get back on track when things get out of hand.

12. **Think about the problem while you are doing something that doesn't take all of your attention.** You can have a flash of genuine inspiration while you are relaxing, taking a shower, driving the car, or exercising.

13. **Ask your friends for suggestions.** They may have some interesting new ideas, and their input may help you think about the problem differently.

Let's look at some teaching dramas that illustrate the brainstorming process. The first one was taken from the practice exercises in the previous chapter.

The Problem. Will is 15, and he wants to have his friend, Tom, stay overnight. The last time this happened, however, the CD player in Will's bedroom could be heard all through the house late into the night. When Dad finally tried to get the boys to turn off the CD player, there was a terrible fight that woke up the whole family. Dad and Will ended up shouting and slamming things around, and Dad cut the plug off the cord to the stereo with some pliers.

As you break down a problem like this, the first step is to remove the emotional debris and focus on the goal statement. Quite simply, Will's goal is to have a friend stay overnight. The next step is to defuse the negative emotions that are associated with the issue. One way to do this, as we mentioned earlier, is for Will to assume some responsibility for the problem. Will may think the fight was his dad's fault, but it is unlikely that he will achieve his goal by pursuing this point. Another approach Will could take is to begin his presentation with an apology. The next step would be to work with the family to develop a plan to prevent the problem from occurring again.

Act I: It Won't Happen Again, I Promise

The Scene. Mom and Dad are sitting in the living room with Will and his 11-year-old sister, Marti. The conversation begins as Will makes his pitch.

Will: I know that the last time I had Tom over, we created a scene by playing music late at night. (looking very sincere) I'm sorry about that, I *really* am. If I were you, I would think twice about ever letting me have a friend stay overnight again. But I would appreciate it if you would give me another chance. I'd like to have Tom stay the night next Saturday. I promise that there won't be a problem this time.

Mom: That was well said, Will. Who would you like to "receive" your message?

Will: It should be Dad, since he's the one who was so angry.

Dad: You're right about that. I *was* angry. But I'm impressed with how well you seem to understand my point of view. You admitted that you created a scene by turning up the CD player full tilt, and you realized that we are likely to say no to having friends come over again. In spite of all this, you would like to have Tom stay here on Saturday night.

Will: Yes, that's it, exactly. Except you forgot my promise.

Dad: Oh, that's right. This time you say there won't be a problem.

Will: Yes. I promise!

Dad: You promise. Now let me present my side.

Mom: OK, but first let's take a break so that you can think about the *one* piece of information you want to add from your point of view.

Dad: That's a good idea. Let's take five.

They set the timer for five minutes and take a break. Dad considered several of the comments he could make. He would like to complain about the sleep he lost last time and how upset he was for two or three days afterward. Furthermore, there was the well-being of the rest of the family to consider. But since Will was so grown up in the way he made his request, Dad wanted to be reasonable.

After thinking carefully about the problem, Dad decided that his goal was to find a way to deal with situations like this in the future, and he knew that bringing up the past would impede progress. Finally, Dad figured that the best way to achieve his goal was to have the family generate a set of house rules that would be followed when visitors spend the night. When the timer bell sounded, the family reassembled in the living room.

Notice that Dad's presentation is particularly effective because he shows that he understands Will's perspective by humorously reflecting on his own teenage years.

> **Dad:** I want you to know that I, too, was a boy once upon a time. And, if the truth were known, I guess I made a mistake or two when I was your age. So I am willing to *consider* your request, but first I want to establish some house rules for times when there are visitors.
>
> **Will:** (smiling) You made mistakes when you were a boy, so you will consider letting Tom come over again. But first we have to make some rules. Is that right?
>
> **Dad:** Yes, son. You hit the nail on the head. I'd like a list of house rules. I think your mother should have some say in this, too.
>
> **Will:** Well, Mom, what do you think?
>
> **Mom:** (thoughtfully) I guess I'd be willing to try it again, but only if we also set some consequences for breaking the new rules.
>
> **Will:** So you want some consequences, too.
>
> **Mom:** Right.
>
> **Dad:** OK, but I think we should work on rules first.
>
> **Mom:** That sounds reasonable to me.
>
> **Will:** Who should write them down?
>
> **Marti:** I will! (She takes the pad and pencil and sits poised for action.)

Commentary

The family was receptive to Will's request because he took responsibility for his prior mistakes. Can you imagine how they would have responded if Will had omitted this step and simply made the request? Dad moved the discussion forward by suggesting that some new house rules were needed to deal with the situation. Then Mom added the stipulation that some consequences should be established for violating the rules. With Marti as note taker, the family begins brainstorming.

Mom: Before we get started, we should decide on a strategy. As I understand it, the first step is to come up with a set of rules. Is that correct?

Dad: Yes. And then we will set some consequences for rule violations.

Mom: So we'll follow the brainstorming guidelines and come up with as many rules as we can. Then we'll select a few of them to try out.

Will: Does that mean that Tom can come over this weekend?

Dad: Maybe—it all depends on whether we can work together and finish setting up these rules and consequences. If all goes well, I may be willing to give them a pilot test. What about you, Mom?

Mom: I guess so.

Dad: And, Marti, would you be willing to give Will another chance? Remember, you might be in his place some day.

Marti: Can I just stay over at *my* friend's house and not even be here?

Mom: (smiling) We'll talk about that later. But right now we need an answer to your father's question.

Marti: I guess Will should have another chance.

Dad: Then let's begin. I think the first rule should be lights out and no noise after 10 P.M.

Will: (looking alarmed) Come on, Dad, that's my bedtime on school nights! Let's be reasonable.

Mom: I know that sounds terrible to you, Will. But keep in mind that anything goes during brainstorming. You will have a chance to help us evaluate the suggestions later. Marti, write that down.

Marti: (begins writing) OK.

Mom: How about this—you can stay up until midnight if you're quiet.

Will: Let's make that 1 A.M.

Dad: Since your CD player is right next to our bedroom wall, let's make a rule that there will be no music after we go to bed. If you must have music, it will be played quietly in the family room, where it won't bother anyone.

Marti: Slow down, you guys. I can't keep up with you. (She talks aloud as she writes.) Bedtime is 1 A.M. After Mom and Dad go to bed, music can only be played quietly in the family room.

Dad: No phone calls, either in or out, after 10 P.M.

Will: How about only *outgoing* phone calls after 10 P.M.

Mom: I would like to suggest only two warnings before a consequence is applied.

Dad: That's a good idea. Maybe we should work on some consequences now.

Mom: Not unless we're done with the rules. Does anyone else have some more rules to suggest?

Marti: I do. I want both Will and Tom to be polite to me.

Will: Oh, come on, Marti, we *are!* You're the one who makes life difficult.

Mom: Just write it down, Marti.

Dad: Are there any other rules? (Everyone is silent.) Going once, going twice . . . OK, the brainstorming session is officially over.

Commentary

You may have noticed that this family started out by planning a strategy. First they wanted to develop a list of rules and then discuss the consequences. Will was relatively successful in getting everyone to agree that Tom could come over on Saturday, but Mom and Dad wisely imposed the when/then rule to encourage Will to cooperate: *when* the rules and consequences were spelled out, *then* a friend could spend the night.

It is a good idea to keep the guidelines for brainstorming handy so you can refer to them if necessary. During the brainstorming session, people may violate these guidelines. After two violations, start recording them. Simply list everyone's name, and keep score. Don't argue about the violations, just record them. In the last scene, Will violated the rule about evaluating suggestions twice, but these offenses were not labeled or written down. You might want to make a rule that people with three strikes against them must leave the discussion for five minutes.

After you have made a list of possible solutions, read it out loud and ask if changes or additions are needed. Here is what Marti's list looks like:

1. Lights out by 10 P.M.
2. No noise after 10 P.M.
3. Lights out at midnight.
4. Bedtime at 1 A.M.
5. No music after someone goes to bed.
6. After Mom and Dad go to bed, music can only be played quietly in the family room.
7. No phone calls in or out after 10 P.M.
8. Only outgoing calls after 10 P.M.
9. Two warnings and then a consequence.
10. Both Will and Tom will be polite to Marti.

Now that the brainstorming session about rules is over, we will freeze the action and come back to it in the next chapter. In the meantime, let's look in on another family as they try to work on a different type of issue.

Act I: Painting a Pretty Picture

The Scene. The Goodwins are dealing with an issue that evokes strong feelings in some families. Their only child, Polly, wants to wear makeup. Polly is now 13 years old, and she has been wearing makeup away from home for quite a while, but her parents were not aware of this until recently. One day, when Dad was out of town, she wore makeup at home to see how her mother would react. Mom thought it was reasonable. When Dad came home, however, he was very unhappy to see Polly wearing "war paint." Even though Mom and Dad are in mild disagreement about this issue, they have always been able to work through their differences with decorum.

The family is in the car on their way to Grandmother's house, which is a 30-minute drive. The Goodwins often have family problem-solving discussions while they are riding in the car. It seems to work well for them because there are few interruptions. They have already completed the process of describing the problem and sharing perspectives. Now they are ready for the brainstorming stage. Dad has agreed to record the proposed solutions in their agreement notebook, which they have brought along for this purpose. Mom is driving, and Polly is in the backseat.

Mom: Let me sum up the issue and each of our positions. Polly wants to wear makeup, and Dad and I are slightly divided on the issue. Dad doesn't want to allow any makeup at all, and I think that a little might be OK. Am I right?

Polly: Yes.

Dad: That's right.

Mom: Good. Now we need to think of some ways to compromise.

Polly: You guys could just let me wear makeup.

Mom: You mean, whenever you want?

Polly: Yes. And as much as I want. After all, it's *my* face.

Dad: Hmmm. (shakes his head while he begins writing) You know what I think about that, but I'll write it down anyway.

Mom: Remember, we're not supposed to disagree at this point.

Dad: Yes, I know. I'll try to control myself.

Mom: We could allow her to wear makeup for special occasions.

Polly: Maybe you'd let me wear it to school, too, if I only use a little.

Dad: I don't want you to wear any makeup at all until you're a reasonable age, like 18.

Polly: (whining) But Dad, I'll be halfway to my grave when I'm 18!

Mom: (laughing) Then I must be a dead woman. You're riding in a car being driven by a corpse.

Polly: (sarcastically) Ha, ha, ha.

Dad: Polly, that's a zap.

Polly: And don't forget to mark down *your* rule violation.

Dad: What was that?

Polly: You disagreed with an idea.

Dad: (cheerfully) OK, OK, I'll keep score on the put-downs. (He starts writing.)

Mom: Let's get back to the brainstorming. How about waiting until you're 15 or 16? I'll bet that would make Dad happy.

Polly: How about letting me wear makeup for good behavior? After all, I *am* a straight-A student.

Mom: She has a good point there.

Dad: I am proud of you for the grades you get. I'll write that down.

Mom: Here's a silly idea, just for the record. How about if we insist that when she wears it, she paints herself with makeup three inches thick so she looks like a punk rock star?

Dad: I'd prefer a prettier picture, something sweet like a Barbie doll. (Everyone bursts out laughing as they consider these two extremes.)

Here is the list of solutions the family generated during their brainstorming session:

1. Wear makeup all the time.
2. Special occasions only.
3. Light applications for school.
4. No makeup until 18.
5. No makeup until 16.
6. Allow makeup for good behavior—straight As.
7. Wear three inches of makeup, like a punk rock star.
8. Pretty as a picture, like a Barbie doll.

Commentary

The Goodwins are off to a good start. Mom's summary of the various positions set the stage for productive brainstorming. One of the techniques used by the Goodwins was to consider the extremes in their positions as options—one possibility is wearing no makeup at all, and at the opposite extreme is wearing makeup three inches thick. This technique usually adds a little humor to the discussion, and it is a good way to represent the range of solutions. The next step is to find a compromise position that lies somewhere in the middle.

Did you notice how the Goodwins handled the rule violations and put-downs? After Dad labeled Polly's zap, she reminded him to write down his rule violation, which he did without getting angry or defensive. Then he moved the discussion back on track.

Now that the Goodwins have finished brainstorming about Polly's makeup, we'll freeze the action and return to this issue in the next chapter. In the meantime, let's look in on another family as they work on a different type of issue.

Act I: She Came in through the Bathroom Window

The Scene. The Wright family is in the midst of dealing with a serious issue. Their 18-year-old daughter, Jody, has stayed out all night. She tried to sneak in through the bathroom window early that morning, but she was caught in the act. Everyone was upset at first, so they waited until evening to talk about the consequences for Jody's violation. In the meantime, Mom and Dad have been discussing the issue between themselves. Jody has not talked to anyone about it because she has been grounded and is not allowed to use the telephone.

Mom and Dad are sitting in the living room with Jody and their son, Craig, who is 15. Nobody looks particularly cheerful.

Mom: This meeting has been called to set a consequence for Jody's staying out all night. I know we are all upset, so let's make a special effort to stick to the guidelines for brain-storming. (She places the rules in the center of the table.) Craig, I want you to label rule violations and keep score. Remember to be neutral when you announce violations. I will record the suggestions.

Dad: I'll begin. I think Jody should be grounded for the rest of the school year. This is very serious.

Mom: That's one idea. But that could create problems . . .

Craig: (interrupting) Remember, Mom, you're not supposed to disagree yet. That's rule violation number one for you.

Jody: Maybe I could do a one-hour work chore.

Dad: If you think you're getting off that easy, you're kidding yourself.

Craig: OK, Dad, you get a zap mark, too.

Mom: You and I aren't doing very well, John. Let's work a little harder at this.

Dad: OK, I'm sorry. How about making that five minutes for every minute she was late?

Craig: How about minute for minute?

Mom: How about one day of being grounded for every hour she was late?

Dad: As far as I'm concerned, it should be more like a week for every hour.

Jody: How about writing an essay on the evils of staying out all night?

Dad: Let's make it a page for every minute she was late.

Mom: I think one page for every hour would be more reasonable.

Craig: How about making Jody do her chores *and* my chores for a month?

Jody: (meekly) Would it help if I apologize?

Dad: It wouldn't hurt. (Feeling less tense, he tries a joke.) But a little torture might be more appropriate. We could pluck the hairs from her head, one at a time.

Craig: You guys are getting a little weird.

Mom: Write it down anyway. Dad just wants to make the punishment fit the crime.

Jody: Oh, come on, it wasn't a *big* crime. You wouldn't even have known if you didn't happen to get up so early.

Dad: (With self-righteous anger, he raises his voice.) That is *not* the issue. You stayed out all night doing who knows what!

Mom: OK, Craig, you'd better write that down as a rule violation. Remember to stay calm, Dad. We're thinking about how to punish her.

Craig: What about losing phone privileges for a week?

There is a long, heavy silence. Nobody seems to have any new ideas.

Mom: Let's put this list up on the refrigerator. If anyone can think of some more ideas, write them down. We'll meet again tomorrow for round two.

Here is their list:

1. Grounding for the rest of the school year.
2. A one-hour work chore.
3. Work chore—five minutes for every minute late.
4. Work chore—minute for minute.
5. Grounding—one day for every hour late.
6. Grounding—one week for every hour.
7. Write an essay.
8. Essay—one page for each minute late.
9. Essay—one page for each hour late.
10. Do own chores *and* Craig's.
11. Apologize.
12. Torture—pluck out one hair at a time.
13. Lose phone privileges for a week.

Commentary

Jody has reached the age of majority. At 18, she could legally live on her own, but no one really wants her to leave. On the other hand, since she *does* live at home, she enjoys many luxuries that she could not afford otherwise. While Jody is living at home, she is accountable for her actions and must face the consequences for rule violations like anyone else in the family.

This situation has disrupted the entire family, and everyone would like to put closure to the issue by coming up with a reasonable consequence. The consequence needs to be small enough that it doesn't drag on forever, yet unpleasant enough to prevent the problem from occurring again. All too often, parents assume that discipline will work only if children really suffer. But in the long run, intense punishment doesn't work; it just creates resentment. Most teenagers have a strong sense of fairness, and they are willing to accept reasonable consequences. They also need to know that their parents will impose a consequence when they do something inappropriate.

It was a good idea for the family to postpone the brainstorming session for a day or two because nobody knew what to do. Jody had always been a well-behaved child, and this was her first notable act of disobedience. But it was also serious. Who knows why she stayed out all night? The parents decided that even if drugs, alcohol, or sex were involved, the best course of action would be to set a consequence and come up with a plan for preventing the problem in the future. They consulted their friends, and so did Jody.

During the next couple of days, the following suggestions were added to the list:

14. Assess a fine for time overdue.
15. Lock her out of the house the next time she's an hour or more late.
16. Take away her driving privileges.
17. Forgive her if she promises never to do it again.
18. Have her check in when she comes home late.
19. Have her write down her time of arrival and leave it in the kitchen before going to bed.

This teaching drama will not be concluded for you. Instead, your family will evaluate this list of consequences as part of the homework assignment in the next chapter.

Key Ideas in This Chapter

1. Brainstorming means working together to generate a list of possible solutions to a problem.

2. Everyone's perspective should be represented.
3. Brainstorming is a good way to find effective solutions to difficult problems.
4. Offer support for people's suggestions.
5. The guidelines for brainstorming provide the structure necessary to foster a spirit of cooperation and prevent negative emotions from interrupting the process.

Chapter Two Homework Assignment

1. Call a family meeting to practice communication skills, and then try brainstorming.
2. Start by presenting and receiving information about family issues using the practice exercises provided below. Switch roles occasionally so that the adolescent sometimes plays the part of the parent and vice versa.
3. If everyone seems to be doing well with presenting and receiving, try brainstorming some solutions. Complete steps #4 and #5 before you start.
4. Ask someone to volunteer to keep track of rule violations. This person should write the name of each family member on a sheet of paper. When a rule is violated, it is this person's job to briefly label it by saying something like "Dad, you're not supposed to criticize ideas, that's a violation for you." Then a mark should be made next to Dad's name on the sheet of paper.
5. Have someone else record the solutions that are generated during the brainstorming session. This person should write down every idea suggested.
6. Now you are ready to try brainstorming by using the practice exercises provided below. Go through the exercises twice. The first time you do this, try to violate as many of the guidelines as possible. Make sure the person who is recording violations writes them down and gives appropriate feedback to offenders. Then go through the exercises again, but this time practice brainstorming without violating the guidelines. Remember: When you are in the brain-

storming stage, don't stop until you have at least five suggestions on your list.

7. Save these records for the next meeting.

Practice Exercises

1. You have received a call from school because your son is talking back to teachers and arriving late to classes. This is the third time this year you have received a call like this. You want to stop this behavior before it becomes even more serious. What should the consequence be?

2. Your daughter has been coming home late on school nights. This has now developed into a habit. The first time you didn't do anything about it because she was only 15 minutes late. The next time she was 30 minutes late, and you let that go, too. Last night she was an hour late. You want her to come home on time. Develop some solutions that include positive consequences for being on time as well as punishment for being late.

3. You are 16 and have kept a personal diary for several years. One day you discover that someone has been reading your diary. You want to find out who is doing this, and you want some assurance that it won't happen again.

4. You are a 17-year-old with a driver's license. You would like to be able to drive the family car on a weekend night.

5. There are several teenagers in the family, and they are forever fighting about the telephone. One of the main issues is that when the telephone rings, everyone runs for it. This means that the telephone is often answered by someone who is out of breath, giggling furiously, or shouting at siblings to get away. You want the phone answered in a polite and orderly way.

Guidelines for Brainstorming

1. Involve everyone in the process.
2. Take turns.

3. Come up with at least five possible solutions.
4. Encourage creativity.
5. Do not evaluate ideas.
6. Record *every* suggestion, even if it seems ridiculous.
7. Do not allow criticism or hostility.
8. Be neutral about the ideas you dislike.
9. Use humor occasionally.
10. Write down rule violations.
11. If the discussion becomes heated, take a five-minute break or postpone the session until later.
12. Think about the problem while you are doing something that doesn't take all of your attention.
13. Ask your friends for suggestions.

CHAPTER 3

Evaluating Solutions

This stage in the problem-solving sequence ties together the loose ends from the previous steps. The process of evaluating solutions enables the family to decide on a rational course of action by considering in advance the positive and negative aspects of each solution. Each viable option is discussed, and its advantages and disadvantages are listed. Now family members can express negative opinions without getting into a fight because their comments are directed at solutions, not people. If someone wants to champion an idea, he or she must point out its benefits. The list of viable options is gradually narrowed down until one or two ideas emerge as the most promising. Then an agreement is drawn up based on these ideas, and it is put into action on a trial basis.

There are a series of questions to consider during the evaluation process. How might this choice affect the family? Would it be difficult to implement the plan and follow through consistently? What are the possible side effects? How would the various family members feel if one course of action was followed versus another? Will the plan solve the problem? These and other questions are addressed during the decision-making process.

Although the procedure for evaluating solutions is based on group process, it is the responsibility of the parents to guide the final decision. Adolescents and other children tend to focus on short-term goals, and their input often reflects this approach. Parents, on the other hand, should emphasize long-term objectives.

The way in which the final solution is handled depends on how open the parents are to input from their children and the nature of the problem being considered. Some parents run relatively democratic households; others feel it is necessary to maintain more control. Decisions about how to handle serious rule violations tend to be made primarily by parents, and less critical matters are usually decided by the entire family.

When group process is used to evaluate solutions, each member of the family suggests at least one advantage and one disadvantage for each of the ideas on the list. It is important to conduct an orderly discussion and to take notes on the points that are made. Begin by reading the list of options out loud, and try to eliminate the ones that everyone agrees are not workable. Then consider each of the remaining alternatives one at a time. Take turns so that everyone has a chance to propose advantages and disadvantages. Keep your mind open as the discussion unfolds. Sometimes the best parts of two or more ideas can be combined to arrive at a solution that is agreeable to everyone.

This process of evaluating solutions by anticipating their potential impact is useful, but the final test is how well the solution works. Simple problems often have straightforward remedies. The solutions to complicated issues, however, may require some fine-tuning. In some instances it may be necessary to break the problem down into smaller components. If you are working on academic performance, for example, the first step is to develop a plan to establish effective study habits; good grades will follow later. Once you have decided on a course of action, a contract is drawn up to spell out the terms of the agreement. The contract underscores the family's commitment to change. The solution is then tested for a week or two.

Typically, contracts must go through several revisions before the plan is operating smoothly. As you reevaluate how well the "solution" is working, several questions should be addressed. Which parts of the plan are working and which are not? Are there any surprising benefits or negative side effects? How do people feel about the way things turned out? Who is affected and how? Can you learn from your mistakes and make improvements? The process of refining the terms of your agreement is guided by these questions.

The following steps outline the procedure for narrowing down the list of possible solutions.

Steps for Evaluating Solutions

1. **Examine the list of solutions.** Are there some ideas that clearly won't work? Is there an outlandish suggestion that was intended to provide comic relief or a solution that could have disastrous consequences? Now is the time to eliminate these options from the list. Begin by handing out pieces of paper and having each person indicate which ideas are not worth considering.

2. **Eliminate the solutions that everyone agrees will not work.** Don't pressure people to change their opinions at this stage.

3. **Discuss the advantages and disadvantages for the remaining ideas.** Each person is expected to suggest a minimum of one advantage *and* one disadvantage for each solution. Even if you dislike a particular idea, think of some of the benefits it may have. To do this, you may have to consider it from another person's perspective. If you favor a certain option, make a case for it by spelling out its positive qualities.

4. **Record the pros and cons for each option.** Use a separate sheet of paper for each solution. Briefly describe the solution at the top of the page, and have someone in the group record the pros in one column, and the cons in another.

5. **A consideration that is viewed as an advantage for one person may be a disadvantage for someone else; if this is the case, record it in both columns.** Let's say, for example, that the issue is an adolescent's habit of coming home late for din-

ner. One of the proposed solutions on the list is to let the adolescent earn extra telephone privileges for being on time. Mom points out that this would make it more difficult for everyone else to use the telephone, which she considers to be a disadvantage. Dad, on the other hand, hates getting calls in the evening, so he sees this as an advantage. Under the solution "earn extra telephone time," the comment "ties up the line" would then be listed in both the pro and the con columns.

6. **Be brief. Make your comments short and to the point.** Otherwise, the discussion will drag on and people will become frustrated.

7. **Accept what people say and record their comments in the appropriate column.** Refrain from criticizing each other. Your comments should be directed at the solutions being evaluated.

8. **Consider each person's point of view.** This is the goal of group process.

9. **After you have examined each solution using the steps previously outlined, try to narrow the list.** Once again, have family members indicate which of the solutions they would like to remove from the list. Eliminate only those ideas that everyone agrees will not work.

10. **If there are still more than one or two solutions on the list, think again about the pros and cons for the remaining ideas.** Discuss how each solution might change family life. Would it resolve the underlying issue? Would it create new problems? A well-conceived plan takes all of these aspects into consideration.

11. **If you still can't reach an agreement on which solution you should try, return to the brainstorming stage.** Perhaps there is a way to approach the issue that has been overlooked (see #14).

12. **Be willing to try out an idea even if it isn't perfect.** If the solution with the most support has any promise at all, give it a chance. You don't have to try anything for more than one week at a time, and you may develop a better understanding of the problem in the process.

13. **Consider combining ideas.** Sometimes you can use parts of two or more ideas to create yet another solution. This can also be a very effective way to arrive at a compromise that satisfies everyone.

14. **If you simply cannot reach an agreement, end the meeting and set another time to try again.** Try not to feel defeated or anxious about arriving at a solution. Difficult problems are usually old ones. If an issue has been around for a while, it may take some time to find a solution. You may want to discuss the issue with friends to get some fresh ideas.

Now let's return to the teaching drama about Will and his family to illustrate how to use these steps for evaluating solutions. As you may recall, Will wanted to have his friend stay overnight. Since there was a problem the last time Will was allowed to do this, his parents want to develop a set of house rules that establish guidelines for conduct and consequences for violations when friends stay overnight. The list of rules they generated during their brainstorming session appears below.

1. Lights out by 10 P.M.
2. No noise after 10 P.M.
3. Lights out at midnight.
4. Bedtime at 1 A.M.
5. No music after someone goes to bed.
6. After Mom and Dad go to bed, the music can only be played quietly in the family room.
7. No phone calls in or out after 10 P.M.
8. Only outgoing calls after 10 P.M.
9. Two warnings and then a consequence.
10. Both Will and his friend will be polite to Marti.

Act II: Setting Rules for Overnight Guests

The Scene. A family meeting has been called into order, and everyone is sitting around the dinner table.

Mom: Let's all write down the rules that can be eliminated. Here is some paper.

She passes around small pieces of paper to use as ballots. The list of proposed rules is passed around the table as family members make their decisions. Marti collects the papers and looks them over carefully before she makes an announcement.

Marti: The only suggestion we can cross out is #1—lights out by 10 P.M.

Mom: OK. Good, that's a start. Marti, please draw a line through that rule. Let's move on to assign priorities to each of the remaining options. (She again passes out some little slips of paper.) Make two columns. On the left side write the numbers 2 through 10 to represent each of the rules on our list. Then write a priority score next to the four rules you think are best. Use a "1" for the rule you like the most, a "2" for the rule you like second most, and so on.

When everyone is finished, Marti again gathers the pieces of paper. Then she writes all of the priority scores next to each of the rules on the master list. Notice that the scores are tallied in such a way that each person's input is essentially anonymous, which means the rules are considered on the basis of merit rather than politics. When Marti is done, the master list is passed around so everyone can look at the results.

Priorities	**Rules**
1, 1, 2	2. No noise after 10 P.M.
2	3. Lights out at midnight.
1, 3	4. Bedtime at 1 a.m.
——	5. No music after someone goes to bed.
2	6. After Mom and Dad go to bed, the music can only be played quietly in the family room.
3	7. No phone calls in or out after 10 P.M.
3, 3, 4	8. Only outgoing calls after 10 P.M.
4, 4, 4	9. Two warnings and then a consequence.
2, 1	10. Both Will and his friend will be polite to Marti.

Dad: I have an idea. Let's begin by accepting the rules that have received at least two priority scores of 1 or 2.

Mom: (Looking thoughtfully over the list, she begins to nod her head.) OK, that seems good to me. That would be #2, "No noise after 10 P.M.," and #10, "Both Will and his friend will be polite to Marti." I think we also need to add rule #4, which is "Bedtime at 1 a.m." The scores are close on that one, and it seems reasonable for the boys to stay up until 1 a.m. on a weekend night as long as they don't make noise. The real issue here seems to be noise.

Dad: OK. That's all right with me. I was more concerned about noise than bedtime when I suggested 10 o'clock.

Mom: Marti, please make a new list. Put "Rules for Conduct" at the top. Then list the following:
1. No noise after 10 P.M.
2. Bedtime at 1 A.M.
3. Will and his friend will be polite to Marti.
Can we all agree on #9, "Two warnings and then a consequence"? That item got three votes. (Everyone nods in agreement.)

Marti: I'll add that to the list.

Dad: That leaves two issues to negotiate: the CD player, and the telephone. Marti, put "Music quietly in the family room" on the top of a new sheet of paper, and let's go over the pros and cons of that. (As Marti does this, the rest of the family continues.)

Will: One advantage is that we will be quiet, but we can also listen to our music. We'll be happy, and so will everyone else. That seems like a real pro to me.

Dad: That's true. But the disadvantage is that you may be running back and forth into your room to get your CDs.

Marti: He could take his CDs into the family room before 10 o'clock.

Dad: Yes, that's a good way to solve the problem.

Mom: Another disadvantage is that they might start out quiet and then get noisier.

Will: That's where the warnings come in.

Mom: Well, I guess that's true.

Commentary

Notice how they were able to streamline the process by agreeing to accept several options based on priority scores. Sometimes you may have to go through the process of evaluating every item on the list, which is more time consuming. But this isn't always necessary.

This family's goal was to develop a set of house rules, which required a slightly different process than looking for a single solution to a problem. Each issue has different characteristics, and the procedures for brainstorming and evaluating solutions can be modified accordingly.

Mom: It looks like outgoing calls after 10 o'clock is more popular than no calls at all, so let's start there.

Dad: I don't like that idea. The disadvantage is that phones will be ringing all over town late at night.

Will: (in an insolent tone of voice) But *nobody* else goes to bed at 10 o'clock. You're the only one I know who does.

Dad: (irritably) I don't care what you say. I don't believe that other parents like having the phone ring at all hours of the night.

Mom: Cool down, you two. Marti, give both Dad and Will a mark for put-downs. (putting her hand gently on her husband's shoulder, she asks) Can you think of one advantage? There must be something good about the idea. Let's follow the rules here.

Dad: OK, I'll try. Come back to me in a minute so I can think about it.

Will: One advantage is that it would make me happy.

Marti: And I would be happy, because then I could use the phone too.

Dad: That's still a disadvantage as I see it. But an advantage is, if you are on the phone after I go to bed, I wouldn't have to worry about the phone ringing. I like that. Maybe we should make a rule that you *can't* talk on the phone until after I go to bed.

Marti: (sarcastically to Will) That's a switch.

Mom: OK, Marti, give yourself a put-down mark for that.

Commentary

It is important to guard against hostile remarks during every stage of problem solving. They simply aren't necessary, and they disrupt the spirit of cooperation that moves the process along. Parents and children alike resent having their negative behaviors labeled, but it should be standard procedure.

Dad: At this point, I would like to say that I am not persuaded to allow phone calls after 10 o'clock.

Mom: Does anyone have an advantage to add that might change his mind?

Will: (whining) Why do we always have to do things his way?

Mom: Do you want to have Tom stay over on Saturday night?

Will: Yes.

Mom: Well then, you better play along or give up on the idea.

Marti: Couldn't we talk about the rules for phone calls some other time?

Dad: I'm willing to talk, but you will have to do some convincing to get me to change my mind.

Marti: Don't worry. I plan to work on this problem, because I'd like to be able to make calls until 11 o'clock on weekends. But this is Will's issue, so I'll wait.

Dad: Will, are you prepared to accept the rule on telephone use?

Will: (looking disappointed) Yes, I can live with it if Tom can come over this weekend.

Mom: Marti, add that to your list of rules, "No phone calls in or out after 10 P.M." If you guys show us that you can be responsible this weekend, maybe your dad will reconsider the telephone issue. But let's try it this way for now.

Commentary

The family has produced a list of house rules that apply when guests stay overnight. A list like this should be considered a first draft. After the rules have been tested, the family may want to add some new rules or modify the original ones.

The family agreed to meet the next day to discuss the consequences for rule violations. They posted a suggestion list on the refrigerator door. That will give them a start for their next meeting.

Now let's return to Polly and her family to see how they are doing with the issue of wearing makeup.

Act II: How Much Makeup Is Too Much?

The Scene. The visit to Grandmother's house has been fun, and everyone is in a good mood. Polly was talkative, cheerful, and polite, and both parents were proud of her grown-up behavior. The whole family baked YuleKaka together, a special kind of Christmas bread that has been a symbol of the holiday season on Mom's side of the family for generations. Even Dad was involved in the preparations. As they drive down the road, Dad takes a pen in hand and mediates as the family decides what to do about allowing Polly to wear makeup.

Dad: Let me read the list of ideas we have developed so far:
1. Wear makeup all the time.
2. Special occasions only.
3. Light applications for school.
4. No makeup until 18.
5. No makeup until 16.
6. Allow makeup for good behavior—straight As.
7. Wear three inches of makeup, like a punk rock star.
8. Pretty as a picture, like a Barbie doll.

Mom: Are there any ideas we can agree to eliminate?

Polly: Yes, I'd like to scratch three of them: no makeup until I'm 16, no makeup until I'm 18, and the one about wearing it three inches thick.

Mom: I agree with you on all three. (turns to Dad) What do you think?

Dad: (He shrugs his shoulders, shakes his head, and smiles.) What can I say? If I don't agree with the two of you, you might gang up on me until I give in. But I'd like to eliminate wearing makeup to school.

Polly: But school is *the* most important! I don't want to go around looking like a dog.

Mom: I guess we better keep that one on the list, because we aren't unanimous. Let's start with "Wearing makeup to school."

Commentary

After you eliminate as many ideas as possible, select one of the remaining suggestions to get the discussion rolling.

Polly: On the pro side, I would look like all the other kids, instead of sticking out like a sore thumb.

Dad: But a disadvantage is that people would be responding to how you look, not who you are. Beauty's only skin deep, you know.

Polly: (She rolls her eyes and sighs. She has heard that line a dozen times.) I know, I know.

Mom: It would give Polly more self-confidence. It's important to feel good about yourself at 13.

Polly: (Her enthusiastic response shows that she appreciates the support.) That's right!

Mom: But a disadvantage is that she could become vain.

Dad: (He nods his head while writing furiously.) That's one of the things I'm worried about. Also, I'm concerned that she will look cheap, and I know how guys talk about girls who wear heavy makeup.

Commentary

Sometimes children become petulant when they think they might not get their way. Teenagers with a little more savvy try to create a good impression.

Polly: Wearing makeup doesn't make a girl look *cheap.*

Mom: Not if you are subtle about it. (turns to Dad) After all, you don't complain about me wearing makeup.

Dad: That's because you don't wear it. (Mom and Polly both laugh knowingly.)

Mom: I can't believe you never noticed. After all these years? Are you serious?

Dad: (looking a little embarrassed) All right, I guess I'm not an authority on makeup. You're telling me that you wear makeup. Are you wearing it now?

Mom: Yes, I am. I wear it whenever I leave the house, even to go to the store.

Dad: Well, you always look good to me. Maybe a little makeup doesn't make an older woman look cheap.

Mom: (She chuckles at this.) Let's not change the subject—*my* age is not the issue here. I guess if we decide to let Polly wear a little makeup to school, we will have to define what that means. But let's move on to some of the other ideas.

Dad: All right. Let's try "Allow makeup for straight As."

Polly: I think it's a good idea to let me earn the right to wear makeup, but do I have to get straight As?

Dad: Why not?

Polly: Because I do get Bs sometimes, and it wouldn't be fair to punish me for that. I still have an outstanding grade point average.

Dad: OK, let's make that a B+ average.

Mom: That sounds more reasonable. What do you think, Polly?

Polly: Does that mean I get to wear makeup?

Dad: Let's not rush things here!

Commentary

Notice how the standard for earning the right to wear makeup was shifted from straight As to a B+ average, which was a good compromise. As you discuss various solutions, they can be changed to reflect the consensus of the group.

Polly: Well, a disadvantage is that if I want to be sneaky, you'll never know if I am wearing makeup at school.

Mom: I could find out—I have my ways. But you're right, you would be tempted to disobey the rule if we say no.

Dad: An advantage is that you would be motivated to keep up the good work in school, and that's important to me.

Mom: But she already does. The biggest problem is her attitude around the house. I'd be willing to let her wear a little makeup to school if she would just have a decent attitude.

Dad: You've got a point there. I guess I would agree to allow a *little* bit of makeup for special occasions if Polly gets good grades and improves her attitude.

Polly: (Her face lights up with a big smile, and she gives her dad a hug.) Oh, Dad. Sometimes you're wonderful!

Mom: OK, you two. Stop the mush or I'll drive off the road. Let's discuss what "a little makeup" means. And do you mean special occasions only or school as well?

Commentary

The Goodwins have finally agreed to let Polly wear a little makeup sometimes. They still have to determine how much makeup is allowed and when it is permitted. After some further discussion, Dad decided to let Polly wear subtle makeup at school for one week, on a trial basis, but only if Polly maintained a good attitude around the house. There had been a lot of conflicts between Polly and her mother lately and if a little makeup would help to solve the problem, he could yield a little. They decided that Mom would keep track of Polly's attitude on a daily basis (guidelines for tracking and monitoring are provided in Chapter 3 of *Part 1: The Basics*). If Polly had a bad attitude on a given day, she would not be allowed to wear makeup to school the next day. And, if Polly was caught wearing makeup when it was not permitted, she would lose telephone privileges for one week.

The next task for the Goodwins is to define how much makeup Polly can wear. They decide to do this by brainstorming definitions. Polly has taken over the role of Recorder.

Dad: To me, "a little makeup" means that you can't tell it's there, like the way your mother does it.

Polly: (defensively) Mom's older than I am, and I want to wear more makeup than that!

Dad: But I don't think 13-year-old girls should wear any makeup at all. You're trying to grow up too fast!

Mom: I have an idea! You can check her makeup every morning before she goes to school and decide whether it's subtle enough.

Dad: I can't do that. Sometimes I leave for work too early.

Mom: Wait a minute here. We have forgotten that we're not supposed to criticize ideas during brainstorming.

Polly: That's right.

Mom: Let's try again, and this time we'll keep track of violations.

Dad: How about this? I'll check it on the mornings if I'm home, and you do it when I'm not. I trust your judgment.

Polly: (in a sarcastic tone of voice) But you don't trust *my* judgment.

Mom: Polly, give yourself a mark for that.

Polly: (complaining) But he doesn't. Neither of you trusts me.

Mom: If you want to talk about trust, let's do it at another time. Right now we are working on the makeup issue.

Polly slumps down in the backseat and shakes her head, but since she is in the backseat, her parents don't see this.

Mom: (to Dad) Do you agree to check Polly's makeup when you're home in the morning before school? I'm willing to do it if you're not there.

Dad: Yes, but remember, this is just for *one week.*

Polly: Can I keep using makeup if I get good grades and get along with Mom?

Dad: Let's see how this works out first. And now, let's draw up a contract to make sure everyone understands what we have agreed to.

Commentary

Notice how this brainstorming session quickly generated the terms of the agreement because the prior stage had laid the groundwork. There were a few rule violations along the way, but when they started recording them this was less of a problem. Polly's attempt to sidetrack the discussion by introducing the topic of "trust" was easily managed by agreeing to talk about it at another time.

There are two more aspects of the discussion that should be mentioned. First, they decided to try the new arrangement for one week, which should motivate Polly to try hard to live up to her end of the agreement. People are usually more willing to compromise if the agreement is only temporary. The second aspect that should be noted is the use of a contract. The importance of this is discussed in the section that follows.

Family Contracts

Writing a contract that spells out the terms of a verbal agreement underscores the commitment to change and prevents misunderstandings. Contracts are a formal statement of the details that emerge during the process of evaluating solutions. The first step is to write a draft of the agreement. This draft should then be discussed so that the terms can be reworded or clauses can be added if necessary. Everyone's perspective should be represented. Dealing with the details at this stage will keep disputes from flaring up later on.

Family contracts are similar to other types of interpersonal contracts. They include the date, the specific terms of the agreement, and the consequences for violations. Everyone involved should sign the contract after it has been approved.

It is important to keep the contract handy so that it can be consulted when questions arise. You may want to put all of your contracts in a special notebook, which then becomes a part of the family's history. Most of us start baby books for our children. Why not keep a contract book to hand down over the generations?

The following are the contracts that were developed by the two families involved in the teaching dramas in this chapter.

Contract: Polly's Makeup

December 4, 2004

Rules for Wearing Makeup:

Polly will be allowed to wear a little makeup to school for one week. At the end of this trial period, Polly's efforts to honor the terms of this contract will be evaluated. The contract will only be extended with the approval of both parents.

Definitions:

"A little makeup" means it is barely visible. Dad or Mom will check Polly's makeup before she leaves for school each day. Dad will do the checking if he is home in the morning; otherwise, Mom will fill in. The decision made by Dad or Mom is final. If it is decided that Polly is wearing too much makeup, she will be given one chance to change her makeup and pass inspection. If Polly's makeup doesn't pass inspection on the second try, no makeup will be allowed for that day.

In exchange for being allowed to wear makeup, Polly agrees to have a good attitude at home. A "good attitude" means being cheerful, responding when spoken to, and being polite. A bad attitude means being grouchy, sarcastic, pouting, and talking back. Mom will keep track of good and bad attitude. If Polly has more than three bad attitude checks during a given day, she will not be allowed to wear makeup to school the next day. If Polly wears makeup when it is not permitted, she will lose telephone privileges for one week.

Signed:
Mom, Dad, Polly

Commentary

Notice how complex this agreement is. For some families, a rough outline is sufficient to prevent misunderstandings. For others, every little detail must be spelled out. Experiment with the contracts you develop to find out how much detail is necessary for your family.

Now let's return to Will's family. They had developed a list of house rules for having a visitor stay overnight, and the next step was to decide on the consequences for rule violations. Their contract includes a list of house rules that can be used generally, and there is a specific agreement for the coming visit.

Contract: When Tom Stays Overnight

October 3, 2004

Will can have Tom over on this coming Saturday night. They agree to follow the rules of conduct described below.

Signed:
Mom, Dad, Will

Rules of Conduct When Visitors Stay Overnight

1. Before 10 P.M. the usual rules apply.
2. After 10 P.M., host and visitor must be very quiet.
3. Music, TV, and other noisy activities are only allowed in the family room after Mom and Dad go to bed (and then quietly).
4. CDs for stereo must be taken into family room before 10 P.M.
5. Lights out at 1 A.M.; no talking after 15 minutes.
6. Will and friend will be polite to Marti and to everyone else.
7. No phone calls in or out after 10 P.M.
8. Two warnings about rule violations before a consequence.
9. Consequences are as follows: first, go to bed, no more talking; second, take visitor home.
10. Failure to comply with this agreement will result in no overnight visitors for three months.

Key Ideas in This Chapter

1. The list of options generated during the brainstorming stage is narrowed down by evaluating each suggestion.
2. The evaluation process is based on considering whether a given solution will solve the problem and how it will affect everyone in the family.
3. Even when group process is used, parents guide the final decision.

4. After selecting a plan of action, record the details of the agreement in a contract.

5. It is usually necessary to revise agreements several times, particularly if the issue is a complicated one. To do this, it may be necessary to return to earlier stages in the problem-solving process. Continue to make changes in the agreement week by week until you have a workable plan.

Chapter Three Homework Assignment

1. Schedule a session to evaluate your list of solutions from the last assignment (brainstorming). Follow the procedures outlined previously. Come up with at least one or two pros and cons per person for each idea. Continue to evaluate the solutions until you reach an agreement or until 15 minutes have passed. If you resolve the issue, write an agreement that describes the details of the plan. If you cannot reach an agreement, post an idea sheet on the refrigerator and have another meeting in two or three days. In the meantime, think creatively about the issue and ask friends for advice. Then evaluate both the old ideas and the new ones. Continue to do this until you reach an agreement.

2. Go through this process for at least two issues with the entire family present so that you have an opportunity to practice evaluating solutions on relatively neutral topics. It will be much harder when you are considering sensitive issues.

3. Evaluate the list of consequences that Jody's family generated in the previous chapter. Explain that Jody was caught sneaking in the bathroom window after staying out all night. The list of possible consequences are as follows (feel free to add some consequences of your own):

    1. Grounding for the rest of the school year.
    2. A one-hour work chore.
    3. Work chore—5 minutes for every minute late.
    4. Work chore—minute for minute.
    5. Grounding—one day for every hour late.

6. Grounding—one week for every hour.
7. Write an essay.
8. Essay—one page for each minute late.
9. Essay—one page for each hour late.
10. Do own chores *and* Craig's.
11. Apologize.
12. Torture—pluck out one hair at a time.
13. Lose phone privileges for a week.
14. Assess a fine for time overdue.
15. Lock her out of the house the next time she's an hour or more late.
16. Take away her driving privileges.
17. Forgive her if she promises never to do it again.
18. Have her check in when she comes home late.
19. Have her write down her time of arrival and leave it in the kitchen before going to bed.

Steps for Evaluating Solutions

1. Examine the list of solutions.
2. Eliminate the solutions that everyone agrees will not work.
3. Next, discuss the advantages and disadvantages for the remaining ideas.
4. Record the pros and cons for each option.
5. A consideration that is viewed as an advantage for one person may be a disadvantage for someone else; if this is the case, record it in both columns.
6. Be brief.
7. Accept what people say, and record their comments in the appropriate column.
8. Consider each person's point of view.
9. After you have examined each solution using the steps outlined above, try to narrow down the list.
10. If there are still more than one or two solutions on the list, think again about the pros and cons for the remaining ideas.

11. If you still can't reach an agreement on which solution you should try, return to the brainstorming stage.
12. Be willing to try out an idea even if it isn't perfect.
13. Consider combining ideas.
14. If you simply cannot reach an agreement, end the meeting and set another time to try again.

Evaluation Form

Description of Issue	
Pros	Cons

CHAPTER 4

The Family Forum

When issues are discussed in a structured meeting, or family forum, it prevents negative emotions from interfering with the problem-solving process. It has been pointed out in earlier chapters that family members often become angry or defensive when they try to work on problems together. People can express their discontent constructively in the family forum while everyone listens and responds appropriately. Group process is the guiding principle, and everyone takes turns presenting issues. Regularly scheduled family meetings make it possible to intervene before problems become serious or difficult to manage, and issues can be resolved instead of letting them pile up. Positive events such as planning fun family activities or announcing someone's achievement can also be presented during the meetings.

If you have read the previous chapters carefully and worked through the homework assignments, you are already familiar with the concept of the family forum. The meetings in which you practiced communication skills, brainstorming, and evaluating solutions were actually mini-forums. Now, these components of the problem-solving sequence are joined together as the structure and inner workings of the family forum are properly introduced.

The family forum is only effective if everyone agrees to abide by a set of rules that spell out how the meetings are conducted and how people should behave. These rules allow family members to participate in the decision-making process in an orderly manner. The following are some recommended guidelines.

Family Forum Guidelines

1. Set a regular time and place for meetings that is convenient for each person's schedule.
2. Have meetings once a week or more often if necessary.
3. Be cheerful and friendly before the meeting.
4. Make the meetings formal, and take them seriously.
5. Work on one problem at a time.
6. Take turns bringing up issues.
7. Assign someone to the role of Recorder to take notes.
8. Assign someone to the role of Mediator to summarize, manage turn taking, and label hostile comments and rule violations.
9. Establish a time limit for the discussion. Start with 15 minutes, and gradually increase the time to no more than one hour.
10. Do not allow phone calls or visitors during the meeting.
11. Stop the meeting if any one person makes more than three hostile comments or rule violations.
12. Observe the communication guidelines presented in Chapter 1.

The first teaching drama shows how the Wrights introduced the idea of the forum to the rest of their family. One night after dinner, the parents announced that they wanted to start having regular family conferences in which they would sit down and consider important issues as a family. Then they asked Craig (15 years old) and Jody (17 years old) to think about when to hold the meetings. It was agreed that the most convenient time was Wednesday nights, after the dinner dishes were done and before TV. They also agreed that everyone would help with the dishes on these nights so they could get an early start. Then they discussed two other basic rules: no visitors and no telephone calls.

Act I: The Wrights Get Off to a Good Start

The Scene. It is Wednesday night, and people have been in a good mood during dinner in preparation for the family meeting. Dinner is over, and everyone pitches in to clear off the table and do the dishes. After a brief flurry of activity, everyone sits down at the table and the discussion begins.

Dad: I'm glad we decided to have meetings to help us get along better. Our goal tonight is to come up with a list of issues to discuss during the next couple of meetings. Before we start, we need a volunteer to write down our decisions. This person is the Recorder for the meeting.

Jody: I'll do it.

Mom: OK, that's great. I bought a new notebook just for this, and, Jody, you get to be the first to write in it.

Craig: So what's the big deal?

Dad: There isn't any big deal. It's just time for us to start working together on some of the things that are bothering people in the family. In order to do that, we have to plan ahead.

Mom: These meetings will give everyone a chance to say what they want to happen in this family. We think you guys should be involved in making some of the rules around here. That will make the rules more fair, and it will reduce the nagging and arguing about them.

Craig: There are lots of things I don't like about this family.

Dad: Maybe so, but the way we are going to do this is to talk about what we *like* and what we *want*. We are going to plan for the future, not get hung up on our mistakes in the past.

Mom: Your dad and I have some rules to help us communicate without getting into arguments. (Mom has a list of rules for family discussions, which she lays on the table.) Who would like to read this out loud? (Nobody answers.)

Dad: OK, I want you guys to take a couple of minutes to read over the list. Your mother and I already know what it says, so we'll come back when you're ready for us to talk about it.

The Wrights used the following set of communication rules to create the structure for their family forum:

Communication Rules

Do
1. Take turns talking.
2. Listen to each other.
3. Paraphrase (that is, restate what the other person has said).
4. Stay on topic.
5. Use humor occasionally.
6. Try to see the issue from the other person's point of view.
7. Summarize the productive parts of the discussion.
8. Treat each other with respect.
9. Be pleasant and friendly.
10. Be brief and to the point.

Don't
1. Lecture.
2. Wander off the topic.
3. Criticize or put down other people.
4. Be rude or disrespectful.
5. Try to read each other's mind.
6. Interpret the meaning behind what people say.
7. Be grumpy, angry, or irritable.
8. Ask, "Why?" (If this is necessary, don't do it during family conferences.)
9. Violate the rules.

After four or five minutes, the parents returned to the table where Craig and Jody were sitting. They went over the list and gave examples of how the rules worked so everyone knew what to expect. Then Dad put some paper and a couple of pencils on the table and asked everyone to write down one or two issues they would like to discuss at a family meeting. When they were done writing, the pieces of paper were collected and put into the notebook. Another meeting was scheduled for the following week, on Wednesday night.

The next teaching drama shows the Wrights dealing with an issue that Craig has raised. Several months have passed since the idea of the family forum was introduced. The family has been meeting regularly on Wednesday nights, and several different problems have been discussed and resolved. They had started with the least emotional issues first and worked into the more difficult issues during later sessions. Their skills have developed with practice, and everyone now understands how the various roles and procedures work in the family forum. Let's look in on them now as they attempt to resolve a tense situation.

Act I: Presenting the Ultimate Outlaws

The Scene. Everyone in the family is sitting around the dining room table. It is family forum night, and it is Craig's turn to present an issue. He has been positively charming for the last two days.

Craig wants to go to a rock concert that is coming to Big City, which is about 100 miles away from Small Town, where they live. His parents don't want him to go, and therein lies the problem. As soon as Craig heard that the Ultimate Outlaws were on tour and coming to Big City, he began to plan his campaign. He has asked to go to rock concerts before, but the answer has always been a very strong no. No matter what approach he's tried, his parents haven't budged on the issue. This time Craig plans to submit his request at the family forum.

Craig has asked his sister, Jody, to be the Mediator for the discussion. The job of Mediator involves keeping people on topic, enforcing the discussion rules, labeling put-downs, and helping the conversation move forward when it gets bogged down. This role is usually assigned to someone in the family who is likely to have a neutral position on the topic. Dad has been selected to act as the Recorder for the meeting. This job entails keeping notes, and writing down ideas and agreements.

Craig is the Presenter, which means he gets to introduce an issue for discussion. Mom's role is that of Receiver. She is the one who is expected to be most opposed to Craig's proposal, so her job is to listen to his statements and paraphrase them.

Craig: (He is trying to look dignified as he gets ready to present his issue, but his nervousness can be seen in the way he bites his lower lip and cracks his knuckles. He begins with a little humor.) Ladies and gentleman, this evening I would like to present the Ultimate Outlaws. They are coming to Big City to entertain those who enjoy heavy metal rock 'n' roll at its finest.

Jody: I may throw up.

Mom: (smiling at Craig's presentation) Jody, you're supposed to be neutral in this discussion.

Jody: Sorry.

Mom: So, the Ultimate Outlaws are coming to Big City.

Craig: Yes. Now, I suspect that you guys may not be dying to see the Outlaws, knowing that you don't like heavy metal, but I want to see them.

Mom: So, you are dying to see the Ultimate Outlaws.

Craig: Yes. You may not think I'm old enough to go to Big City with my friends to a rock concert, but I believe that it's time for you to recognize that I am very mature for my age. I think I can handle it, no problem. After all, I am a very responsible person.

Mom: You want us to consider letting you go even though you know you're too young.

Craig: No, that isn't what I said. I said that you may not *think* I'm old enough yet, but I am mature. And I'm responsible.

Mom: We don't think you're old enough, but you think you are. And you're responsible.

Craig: Right.

Commentary

The purpose of this first meeting was to introduce the issue and to hear the Presenter's point of view. Craig laid his cards on the table. He wants to go to a rock concert in a town 100 miles away.

You may have noticed that the discussion was very structured; the Presenter stated what he wanted, and the Receiver paraphrased his comments. This structure prevents people from responding automatically with negative remarks. The hostile comments, or "zaps," were managed gently yet effectively.

The next stage is to consider the different points of view on the issue.

Jody: So, Craig wants to see the Ultimate Outlaws in Big City, and you and Dad don't want him to go—is that correct?

Mom and Dad exchange meaningful looks. They have been through the rock concert issue before, with Jody, and she was finally given permission to go. They have also discussed it on several occasions with Craig. He was right when he said his parents think he isn't old enough. In a way, they thought Jody was too young as well. They are very concerned about the things that Craig and Jody might be exposed to at rock concerts—alcohol, drugs, people getting high, and sex. There is very little chance that they will let Craig go to the concert, but they are determined to follow the rules of the family forum. If they don't follow through on Craig's issue, the children will lose confidence in the system.

Mom: That's correct.
Craig: That's what I thought.
Jody: Hmmm. (She looks at her father, not knowing exactly how she's supposed to proceed, because she doesn't want to get caught in the crossfire.) Now what?
Dad: Now we're supposed to go around the table, and all of us get to say one thing we think is important about this issue. Craig is supposed to paraphrase.
Mom: I'll start.
Jody: Go for it, Mom.
Mom: From my point of view, rock concerts are full of rowdy people who are using alcohol and marijuana, and all kinds of other drugs. It's no place for children! You can listen to the Ultimate Outlaws at home on your CD player.

Jody: Don't forget, Mom, you can only make one point at a time. Craig, it's your turn to paraphrase what she said.

Craig: (He is so upset by his mother's predictable response that he can hardly control himself, but this is his turn at the wheel and he doesn't want to lose it, so he silently counts to 10 and takes several deep breaths.) Mom is worried about drinking and drugs at rock concerts.

Dad: That's right, son. And that was a good job of paraphrasing.

Craig: Thanks, Dad.

Jody: OK, Dad, what do you want to say?

Dad: Let me see, now. Hmmm. I, too, worry about the problems Mom mentioned, but most of all I worry about transportation—how you will get there, how you'll get home, and who drives.

Craig: Dad is worried about transportation.

Dad: Right.

Jody: Do I get to say what I think, even though I'm the Mediator?

Mom: Sure. It wouldn't be fair if you didn't.

Jody: Well, on one hand, I agree with Craig. I know that rock concerts aren't dens of sin and drugs. But I don't think it would be fair if *he* got to go as a sophomore, when *I* couldn't go until I was a junior.

Craig: Hey, thanks a lot, Jody!

Jody: (sarcastically sweet) Remember to paraphrase, Craig.

Dad: (turning to Jody) And *you* watch your tone of voice.

Craig: (smirking at Jody) Rock concerts are OK for me but not for you.

Dad: Since the Mediator isn't counting put-downs, I will. That was one for Jody and at least one for Craig. Let's take a five-minute break and come back to this.

Commentary

Stage two is well under way. Craig stated the issue in stage one. Then each person made one comment, and Craig paraphrased the various points of view. Calling for a five-minute break was a good idea because it gave everyone a chance to cool off before the discussion became too hot to handle.

Mom calls the meeting back to order after the five minutes are up and begins the final stage of this evening's discussion.

Mom: Our task now is to sum up what has gone on so far, and then we need to gather information about the issue for the next few days. (turning to Dad) Did you write down the different points that have been made so far?

Dad: Yes. Here's what I have. Craig wants to go to Big City to see the Ultimate Outlaws. Mom is concerned about drugs and alcohol, I'm concerned about transportation, and Jody is concerned about whether it's fair for Craig to go to a rock concert as a sophomore when she couldn't go until she was a junior. Did I miss anything?

Dad glances around the table. Craig is looking down at his hands. Nobody has anything to say, so he assumes it's all right to wrap up the meeting.

Dad: When is this concert, Craig?

Craig: Next month, but I have to get my ticket next week if I want to go.

Mom: Oh, boy. I remember the deal about tickets. That's another issue in itself.

Craig: What's the problem?

Mom: That waiting in line all night.

Craig: What's the problem with waiting in line?

Mom: Nothing, so long as it's on your time and it's during the day. But sleeping on the sidewalk is not going to be permitted, and neither is skipping school.

Craig: Can we just save that until after we decide whether I can go?

Dad: (to Mom) He's right. Let's talk about that later. (to Craig) Since we have to move on this pretty quickly, do you want to set another meeting for tomorrow?

Craig: Can't we just finish it now?

Mom: If we do, the answer is no. But I'm willing to think about it overnight.

Dad: How about meeting again tomorrow, after dinner?

Jody: I can't. I have to study for a test.

Mom: Then why don't we have a meeting without you? Do you mind?

Jody: No, that's all right with me.

Dad: OK.

Commentary

Although everyone except Dad "lost it" slightly, this meeting went surprisingly well. Mom and Dad worked together at following the rules, taking turns at gently exerting control when the discussion heated up.

The next step is for the participants to talk to others about the issue. New perspectives may help to break the current deadlock.

Craig's friends, who also want to go to the concert, are pressing the issue with their own families. One of them received permission to go if the other two boys were also allowed to go. One boy's mom said no, but he hasn't given up yet. His tactics are to nag without mercy until she finally gives in. This has worked in the past for him on other issues. Craig has considered using this approach, but he knows that nagging won't work in his family. His best shot is to present a good case in the family forum.

Mom has been talking to her friends. Almost all of the other mothers agreed that they, too, worry about drugs and alcohol at rock concerts. But the consensus seemed to be that sooner or later parents have to allow teenagers to go to rock concerts. The question is, *when* are they old enough? Mom believes that Craig is too young at age 15. She also shares her husband's concern about arranging safe transportation. Her friends suggested that she talk to the other boys' parents about the concert.

Dad asked his friend Bruce for advice. Bruce has kids who are older, so he already has experience dealing with this particular issue. Bruce suggested that they keep the problem-solving discussion focused on the issue of transportation.

Act II: Safety Nets

Dad: Who should be the Mediator tonight, since Jody's not here? Would you feel comfortable with me in that role?

Craig: Sure, I guess so. Just as long as you're fair about it.

Dad: Then let me summarize. You want to go to a rock concert in Big City. Your mom is concerned about drugs and alcohol, I'm concerned about safety on the highway, and Jody is worried about fairness.

Craig: Forget about Jody.

Dad: That's put-down number one. (looking at Mom) What did you find out?

Mom: Everyone I talked to is concerned about drugs.

Craig: Mom, that's just a bunch of bull. There are cops all over the place at rock concerts.

Dad: Craig, that's a zap. (He turns to his wife.) Do you have something to add?

Mom: Yes, I want to know who else is going, and I want to talk to their parents.

Craig: Mom—that went out with the dark ages! I'd die if you called my friends' parents.

Dad: Remember to paraphrase, Craig. What did your mother say?

Craig: She wants to embarrass me to death by calling my friends' moms.

Dad: That's put-down number two. One more, and we stop this discussion.

Craig: Sorry.

Dad: I have a suggestion. What if we take *one* of our concerns and try to solve it? Let's talk about transportation.

Mom: That sounds like a good idea to me. What do you think, Craig?

Craig: OK.

Dad: So let's brainstorm some ways that you could get there and back safely.

Craig: Why can't I just go with my friends?

Dad: (writing in the notebook) So one idea is to go with your friends.

Mom: That's not very reassuring to me. The only one who can drive is Miles, and he just got his license a few months ago.

Dad: (to Mom) That's a violation of the rules for you. Remember, we're not supposed to discuss the disadvantages now. We are just looking for some ideas.

Mom: Sorry. This is hard for me because I don't think he should go at all, so it seems silly to think of *how* he should go.

Dad: (to Craig) Should I count that as another violation?

Craig: No, that's OK. (He smiles at his mother, remembering that he needs to have her on his side in order to go to the concert.)

Mom: Sorry. How about if *we* drive you both ways; although, who knows, it would be a . . . oops, never mind. (She catches herself midstream, before she makes a sarcastic comment.)

Dad: Maybe your friends' parents could drive you there.

Craig: What if Jody drives?

Mom: She's usually pretty busy. What if we hired a limousine? (Everybody laughs at this one.)

Craig: Now that's an awesome idea, Mom. I wouldn't mind going in a black limousine, with one-way windows and a bar in the back. People would think *I'm* the rock star.

Dad: (smiling) You could just stay home, and then you wouldn't need to worry about the transportation.

Mom: Or you could take a bus.

Craig: I think there *is* a bus that's going to the concert! Would you be willing to let me do that?

Dad: Well, let's check that out. But we have some other issues that need to be decided first.

Craig: Maybe I could go with some other kids, someone who has more driving experience.

Dad has written down all of these suggestions. Now that the brainstorming session seemed to be over, he summed things up by reading the list of ideas. The family decided to take a break and resume the discussion tomorrow evening so they could consider the new position. Dad posted the options under consideration on the refrigerator door in case people wanted to add new ideas in the meantime. They agreed that at the next meeting they would go over the advantages and disadvantages of the ideas on the list.

At the next meeting, the family discussed the pros and cons for each of the ideas. Using the process of elimination, they decided that there were two means of transportation that would be acceptable. One was if Craig and his friends were driven to and from the concert by a set of responsible parents. The other was to go by bus but only if there was adult supervision other than just the bus driver. Craig was not very happy with either of these options, but they were the *only* conditions under which his parents would consider the issue further. Craig accepted the idea of going on the bus or riding with someone's parents so they could move on.

Exposure to drugs and alcohol was the next issue to be considered. As they discussed this issue, it became clear that Mom was not only concerned about other people using drugs, but she was afraid that Craig and his friends might drink or use drugs if they went to the concert. Craig wisely focused on his behavior and that of his friends, since there was little he could say or do about the behavior of the other people at the concert.

At the next family meeting, the Wrights evaluated some possible solutions to this problem.

Act III: The Drug Test

The Scene. Mom is the Recorder for this session. She is busy writing down ideas as they come up.

Craig: I could *promise* not to touch the stuff.
  Dad: You could let us do a urine analysis when you get home.
Craig: A what?
  Dad: A urine analysis. You know—we would have you pee in a bottle after you come home, and then we would have it checked for drugs.

Craig: You guys, that's disgusting! Talk about an idiotic violation of privacy!

Mom: Craig, that's a put-down. Let's think of some other solutions.

Craig: I can't think of anything . . . and besides, the real problem is that you guys just don't trust me.

Mom: (ignoring his comment about trust) If you went with a set of parents, they could check you out after the concert and determine whether you're straight.

Craig: Or we could take a rent-a-cop to keep us out of trouble.

Mom: OK, I'll write that down.

Craig: I didn't really mean it, Mom.

Mom: That's all right. I'll write it down, anyway. We're supposed to write down every single idea.

Dad: Maybe someone could go along with you to vouch for your safety and your virtue.

Craig: Like who—you?

Dad: That's an idea! After all, I used to like concerts when I was your age.

Commentary

Even though Craig didn't like the ideas that came up during the meeting, there seemed to be some conditions under which he actually might be permitted to go to the concert. Whether Craig would be willing to accept these conditions was another question.

There was one more topic that needed to be considered, and that was Jody's fairness issue. Jody felt that it wouldn't be fair to let Craig go to a rock concert in another city when she wasn't allowed to go at his age. This was a sensitive issue; Jody felt that she had been discriminated against because she is a girl.

When the parents discussed the issue with Jody, they were up front about their feelings. They agreed that they were somewhat stricter with her and explained that it was because she was the oldest child. Almost all parents, they said, make things harder on the oldest child. They also admitted that they felt it was important to be more protective of a girl. When Jody asked why, they said it was because girls can be more easily taken advantage of than boys. "You mean sex?" Jody asked. Yes, sex—they were afraid Jody might be harassed or get pregnant. No, that didn't mean they didn't trust her. It was just that they were familiar with the temptations of sex in the adolescent years. Yes, they were concerned with Craig's sexual behavior as well, but that was not the issue being discussed right now. Jody still felt discriminated against when the conversation was over, in spite of her parents' best efforts to explain their intentions.

The Wrights had several more meetings on the issue of the rock concert, and it was finally decided that Craig would not be allowed to go. But, as it turned out, Craig's friends couldn't go either. Craig was still upset that he couldn't see the Ultimate Outlaws, but he knew some issues had been resolved during the family meetings that would make it easier for him to go to a rock concert when he was a little older.

Key Ideas in This Chapter

1. The family forum is a structured family meeting that prevents negative emotions from disrupting the problem-solving process.
2. Everyone takes turns presenting issues.
3. It is important to follow the rules for communication and the guidelines for family forums to keep the meetings running smoothly.

Chapter Four Homework Assignment

Designing the Family Forum

In the previous homework assignments you have practiced the skills involved in communication, brainstorming, and evaluating solutions by using practice exercises instead of real issues. In this chapter, you finally get to work on some of the problems in your family by following the steps outlined below.

1. The parents should begin by making a list of the issues *not* open for negotiation. Keep this list as short as possible. Some items may be negotiable in the future as the family gains expertise in solving problems.

2. Introduce the idea of having structured family meetings to make plans, solve problems, and resolve disagreements.
3. Make some copies of the family forum guidelines and rules for communication and discuss them with the rest of the family.
4. From the list of issues you have collected over the past several weeks, select an easy issue and try to resolve it. Assign the role of Mediator to one person who will keep track of rule violations. Assign the role of Recorder to someone else; have that person write down the suggestions generated during the brainstorming session, the pros and cons for each option during the process of evaluating solutions, and the final agreement. Follow all of the problem-solving steps: presenting and receiving information about the issue, brainstorming, evaluating solutions, and writing an agreement.

Family Forum Guidelines

1. Set a regular time and place for meetings that is convenient for each person's schedule.
2. Have meetings once a week, or more often if necessary.
3. Be cheerful and friendly before the meeting.
4. Make the meetings formal, and take them seriously.
5. Work on one problem at a time.
6. Take turns bringing up issues.
7. Assign someone to the role of Recorder to take notes.
8. Assign someone to the role of Mediator to summarize, manage turn taking, and label hostile comments and rule violations.
9. Establish a time limit for the discussion. Start with 15 minutes, and gradually increase the time to no more than one hour.
10. Do not allow phone calls or visitors during the meeting.
11. Stop the meeting if any one person makes more than three hostile comments or rule violations.
12. Observe the communication guidelines presented in Chapter 1 (the communication rules below have been adapted from these guidelines).

Communication Rules

Do

1. Take turns talking.
2. Listen to each other.
3. Paraphrase (that is, restate what the other person has said).
4. Stay on topic.
5. Use humor occasionally.
6. Try to see the issue from the other person's point of view.
7. Summarize the productive parts of the discussion.
8. Treat each other with respect.
9. Be pleasant and friendly.
10. Be brief and to the point.

Don't

1. Lecture.
2. Wander off the topic.
3. Criticize or put down other people.
4. Be rude or disrespectful.
5. Try to read each other's mind.
6. Interpret the meaning behind what people say.
7. Be grumpy, angry, or irritable.
8. Ask, "Why?" (If this is necessary, don't do it during family conferences.)
9. Violate the rules.

CHAPTER 5

Managing Sensitive Issues

It takes skill and courage to manage sensitive issues. When people feel strongly about an issue, the problem-solving process breaks down because emotions get in the way. In families with adolescents, some of the issues that tend to fall into this category are smoking cigarettes, using drugs and alcohol, school problems, experimenting with sex, using the family car, and borrowing personal items from others without asking for permission. When parents and adolescents discuss these issues, the temperature quickly rises. Imposing structure by following the guidelines for communication and using the concept of the family forum will help, but some additional techniques are needed. This chapter describes how to keep the problem-solving process intact by learning better ways to introduce and define sensitive issues.

Setting the Stage for Family Problem Solving

Before you attempt to solve sensitive issues as a family, there are several steps you can take that will help you get off to a good start. The first step is to think carefully about how to define the problem. The second step is to plan how to introduce the problem to the rest of the family. Both steps seem deceptively simple, but there is more involved in doing this correctly than you may think.

Defining the Problem

A good definition should describe the problem so that everyone can recognize when it is occurring. For example, the term "bad attitude" could be interpreted in several different ways because it is not specific enough. A better definition of the problem would break bad attitude into component behaviors such as talking back, testy (irritable) behavior, and constant arguing. These are behaviors that everyone can identify.

A good definition should also identify the problem-solving goals. Let's say, for example, that your teenage daughter is failing in school. Defining the problem as "failing in school" does not identify the goal, which is to do well in school. This goal can then be broken into at least two components: improving work habits at school and establishing a studying routine at home. Now the solution begins to fall into place. One step in defining the problem would be to gather information. It would be a good idea to call your daughter's teachers, for example, to find out about her work habits in class. Does she pay attention when the teacher is talking? Does she follow directions and participate in discussions? Does she get out of her seat and disrupt others? Does she hand in her assignments? If you find that one or more of the above are problems for your daughter, you could then design a program to work on these specific difficulties. The next step would be to keep track of your daughter's studying practices at home. If she is not spending enough time preparing for her classes or is not making good use of the time she spends studying, part of the solution would be to improve her performance in these areas.

Planning a Good Introduction

A good introduction is critical for effective problem solving. The way an issue is presented sets the tone and direction for the discussion that follows: A well-planned introduction will encourage a collaborative effort from family members; a bad introduction leads to conflict, which just creates more problems.

People tend to introduce problems in the worst possible way, because issues usually aren't discussed until there are strong feelings about them. When a problem is presented by someone who is angry, the other members of the family immediately become defensive or disengaged. Everyone knows that getting involved is risky because an angry person is likely to lash out at others who are nearby, even if they are trying to help. Group process is the key to resolving family problems, but this type of introduction makes group participation impossible. The following are some guidelines that will help you get off to a good start.

Guidelines for Good Introductions

1. **Plan ahead.** Give yourself plenty of time to design a good strategy. The problem has probably been around for a while, so it does not have to be solved today, this week, or even this month. It may take the full course of your adolescent's life at home to resolve some of the most difficult issues.

2. **Ask yourself the following questions:**
   a. *When* is the best time to bring up the issue: Right away? After you have cooled off? When people are in a hurry? When everyone is irritable because they are hungry?
   b. *Who* is the best person to talk with first: The person who has created the problem? A friend? Your spouse? One of your children?
   c. *Where* should you introduce the problem: At the dinner table? During a walk? In the car? At a restaurant? In the quiet of the living room? Privately, in the bedroom? During a family forum?
   d. *What* should you say? Think of several alternatives. Make a list of some different ways to introduce the subject. Don't just say the first thing that comes to mind.

3. **Consult with friends.** Get their perspectives on the issue. When you consider which friend to ask, think of someone who is positive and/or someone who especially likes the person involved

in the problem. Pay attention to their positive remarks. Don't depend on depressed friends for advice, because they tend to be cynical or negative, and they may only make matters worse.

4. **If you can, engage a neutral family member as a consultant.** This may be your spouse, an adolescent, or any reasonable person. Don't take the whole problem on your shoulders. You are not alone in the family, although it may feel like it at times.

5. **Practice your presentation.** You can do this either in the privacy of your bedroom, in your car as you are driving, or in the shower. Practice saying it out loud so you can work on your tone of voice. Look in the mirror at your facial expression and body language to make sure you are not sending a negative message.

6. **Be pleasant and calm.** Whenever you can, stay calm. It is even better if you can add a little humor. Laughter is one of the best remedies for a tense situation. Avoid criticizing or expressing negative feelings such as anger, irritation, sarcasm, and hopelessness.

7. **Have a single, simple goal in mind.** Make the goal future oriented. The goal should state what you want. Write it down so you don't forget it.

8. **Accept some responsibility for the issue.** Maybe you haven't been the best role model, or perhaps you have contributed to the issue in some other way. If you can admit some involvement in the problem, other family members may be less defensive and more willing to cooperate.

If the issue is a sensitive one it may be treated like a hot potato, which means that the problem is never resolved. As soon as someone brings up the issue, everyone runs for cover. The hot potato is quickly tossed on the table, and no one dares to pick it up. If an issue is too hot to handle, it should be introduced very carefully. The next teaching drama illustrates the hot potato introduction.

Act I: Where There's Smoke, There's Fire

The Scene. The Blenders are a family of five. Riva is the mother; Ray, her husband of 11 years, works nearly double-time as a small appliance repairman. Riva has a 17-year-old son, Teddy; Ray has a daughter, Alice, who is a 15-year-old high school sophomore; and together, Riva and Ray have a 9-year-old daughter, Meg.

Today, Riva caught Alice smoking a cigarette, which was a blatant violation of the house rule that smoking is not allowed. Alice was hanging out on a street corner with a bunch of rowdy-looking kids when Riva happened to drive by. Alice saw Riva's car, and she knows there will be trouble. There is often trouble between Riva and Alice, partly because Riva is the one who monitors the children and has the unpleasant job of reporting problems to Ray.

The drama begins later that same day, as the family is finishing dinner. Dark clouds seem to hang over the stepmother and daughter, and electricity crackles in the air as it does before a storm. Ray is eating with downcast eyes, hoping that he can finish his dinner before the cloudburst begins.

Riva: Ray, I think we need to have a talk with Alice after dinner.

Ray: I have to go back to work. I'm *way* behind—I promised to finish several jobs by tomorrow and I haven't even started them yet. In fact, I'm already late. (He starts to leave the table.)

Riva: Please don't go now. We *have* to talk. There's a problem with Alice.

Alice: (Her tone of voice matches the hateful look on her face.) The problem is with *you.* If you weren't spying on me, there wouldn't be any . . .

Riva: (interrupting) You shut up! I was talking to your father.

Alice: (muttering under her breath) Witch.

Ray: (becoming angry now, too) You heard your mother. Shut up!

Alice: She's not *my* mother.

Ray: (He raises his voice.) You go to your room right now!

Alice leaves the table in a huff, goes into her room, and slams the door. For a moment there is absolute silence at the table. Then Riva tells the other children to clear the table, and Riva and Ray go into the living room to talk.

Commentary

This situation is complicated because of the stepparenting issues that are involved. If Alice were Riva's daughter, it might be easier for both of them. But when the stepparent has to tell the biological parent that his or her child has done something wrong, it is a sensitive situation. Even though both parents know better, the biological parent often feels personally accused when the stepparent introduces the problem. Let's look at the discussion that takes place between the parents when Riva gives free rein to her anger and hurt feelings.

Act II: Your Daughter, the Tramp

The Scene. Ray glances at his watch and slouches into his favorite armchair. Riva's anger is etched into her face. The statement that Alice made when she stormed out of the room echoes in Riva's mind: "She's not *my* mother, she's not *my* mother. . . ." She has heard these words so often that she has lost count, yet every time Alice throws them in her face Riva feels hurt and angry. The words are especially painful because Riva does most of the direct parenting, but she feels that she gets none of the credit. One look at Ray, and Riva knows that the discussion will turn out like all the others have—Ray will take Alice's side and tell Riva to stop picking on her.

Ray: (Avoiding eye contact, he picks an imaginary piece of lint off his sweater. He wishes his wife and Alice would get along better so he wouldn't have to continually act as the referee between them, and wonders why Riva gets so mad *at him* when Alice screws up—he doesn't want Alice to smoke either. He can't understand why he and his wife end up fighting about things that they agree on. When he finally speaks, he sounds tired and defeated.) So what's the problem this time?

Riva: Don't say it like that. It's not *my* fault *your* daughter creates all these problems. Do you think I like this?

Ray: (He shakes his head slowly and sighs.) No, no, I'm sure you don't. Calm down and tell me what happened.

Riva: She's completely out of control, and I'm really worried that she is heading for serious trouble. She looks like a tramp, and she hangs out on the mall with a bunch of losers. When I saw her today, her face was covered with makeup and there was a cigarette dangling out of her mouth. The next thing you know, she'll come home pregnant!

Commentary

The way Riva has defined and introduced the problem has made it difficult to have a constructive discussion. Instead of engaging her partner, she has pushed him away. Neither of them is thinking about the real goal, which is to steer Alice away from getting hooked on cigarettes.

It is easy to imagine Ray's thoughts. He has few choices, and each of them is unpleasant: he can defend his daughter's virtue, he can launch a full-scale attack on Alice for breaking a house rule, or he can counterattack his wife. Ray knows his life will be miserable regardless of which option he chooses, and he doubts that he can stop Alice from smoking. His parents weren't able to keep him from smoking when he was Alice's age. He would rather just go to work and avoid the whole situation.

Now let's take a look at another way to introduce the problem that enables Riva and Ray to collaborate.

Act III: A Retake for Riva

The Scene. Riva had been thinking about how to bring up the problem ever since she saw Alice looking like a tramp and smoking a cigarette earlier that day. She was concerned that Alice might get herself into trouble by hanging out with a bunch of delinquents, but she knew it would not help to point this out right now. She finally decided to discuss the issue privately with Ray before talking with Alice.

Riva thought carefully about her approach. She practiced her opening statement several times so she could stay calm when she introduced the problem to Ray. She even rehearsed it with a close friend, which helped a lot. Her friend pointed out that Riva was using angry words to describe the problem, and this would force Ray to come to Alice's rescue. Then Riva considered whether she should discuss the problem when Alice was present but decided not to because it would almost guarantee an argument. When issues came up involving Alice, her favorite ploy was to turn Ray and Riva against one another. Riva's next step was to write down her goal—prevent cigarette smoking—to ensure that she and Ray would stay on the topic. They often got sidetracked when they talked about Alice because there seemed to be so many problems to deal with. Riva also admitted to herself that she was not neutral on the subject.

When Ray came home from work, Riva waited for a few minutes before broaching the issue to give him some time to relax and read the newspaper. Alice wasn't home yet, and the rest of the children were in another room, so Riva decided it was a good time to talk to Ray about the problem.

Riva: I know you have to go back to work. I hate to see you working night after night to make ends meet. And I know I'm the one who has to tell you the bad news about Alice. I wish there was some other way to deal with this, but I need your help.

Ray: (cheerfully) Good lord! What has she done now? Robbed a bank?

Riva: (laughing) No, not yet. In fact, I suppose it's not all that serious. But she is smoking cigarettes.

Ray: How do you know that?

Riva: I saw her downtown today smoking a cigarette.

Commentary

In this scene, Riva's introduction is much more effective. The practice sessions made it possible for her to talk about the problem calmly. She also set the stage for a positive response from her husband by showing some appreciation of his hard work and asking for his help. All of her negative comments about the other concerns were censored (how Alice looked, the type of kids she was hanging out with, and what this behavior might lead to). Riva focused on *one* concrete behavior: smoking cigarettes. By keeping her thoughts centered on that, Riva avoided the emotional baggage that had accompanied their attempts to talk about Alice in the past.

With the help of her friend, Riva had *planned her introduction* to obtain the best results, and it worked very well. If you and your spouse have a history of conflict when discussing problems, this may be an important step to take. Talking with someone else can take some of the sting out of an emotional situation if you don't turn these consultations into "bitching sessions." Try to focus instead on the specific steps to take.

In stepfamilies there is frequently the problem of whose child caused the problem. Single parents have their own special problems dealing with children, because there is only one parent to think things through, set the rules, and enforce them. Even when both parents are the biological parents, you often hear complaints prefaced by: "Your son . . ." or "Your daughter . . ."

A good first step is to separate the people from the problem. People are not bad because they have contributed to or caused a problem. The problem is an indication that there are behaviors that must be changed. You have the choice of focusing on behavior or trying to prove that another person is wrong. If you choose the latter, then get ready for a shootout.

Planning the right time and place for the introduction is also important. In the first scene, Riva introduced the problem at dinner with Alice and the other children present. In the last scene, she brought it up when she was alone with her husband. Which approach worked better and why?

It is possible to introduce problems in front of your children if you are skilled and *patient* in your approach. In the next scene, Riva sets the stage for working on Alice's cigarette smoking by getting Ray clearly on her side. She never actually brings up the problem, but she paves the way for success.

Act IV: United We Stand

The Scene. Riva has been in an amazingly good mood, even humming as she prepared dinner. Now that the meal is almost over, she begins to put her winning strategy into motion. Riva has said nothing to Alice about seeing her on the mall, although Alice knows Riva saw her. Her goal is simple: get Ray on her side so they stand together on the issue when it is discussed with Alice. Riva assumes that today was not the first time Alice has smoked, so it won't hurt to take a few days to decide what to do about the problem. She has decided that the best approach is to move slowly and carefully.

Riva: (to Ray) It's been almost a year now since you quit smoking, hasn't it?

Ray: I like to think of it as 327 days. It seems much longer than a year.

Riva: (sympathetically) It was hard for you to quit. I don't know how you did it, because you were so addicted! You couldn't even get out of bed in the morning without a cigarette in your mouth.

Ray: Yeah, it *was* hard. Especially at first.

Riva: I really respect you for it. You said you would do it, and you did! Do you feel any better since you quit?

Ray: I feel a lot better! For one thing, I have more energy. Now I can run up the stairs without sounding like an old locomotive huffing and puffing up the side of a mountain. (Everyone except Alice has a good laugh over that image.)

Riva: Well, I sure hope our kids don't take up smoking. It's a bad habit that's hard to stop.

Ray: Yeah, me too! It would make me feel terrible to see them smoking.

Meanwhile, Alice is looking very uncomfortable. Throughout the conversation, she kept waiting for the boom to fall directly on her head. She can see that Dad would not be happy to hear that she has been smoking with her friends. And she hates Riva because, once again, that witch is going to make trouble between her and her father. But through some miracle, Riva changes the subject pleasantly and the whole issue slides on by.

Commentary

Some people think it is slightly immoral to be strategic with their family. However, these same people don't object to sarcasm, arguing, yelling, or pouting. A little foresight makes it easier to solve family problems. Riva let Alice know that she and Ray are united on the issue. This means Alice has lost her trump card—she won't be able to pit her parents against each other and escape the consequences of violating the rules. Riva's strategy was simple but very effective. She introduced the problem by getting Ray on her side so they could stand together on the issue of cigarette smoking. Let's proceed from where they left off.

Act V: Walking and Talking Together

The Scene. Ray and Riva are taking a walk together. This is an activity that they thoroughly enjoy. There are no kids around to interrupt them, they are relaxed, and they often have good conversations when they go for a walk.

Ray: So, how are things going with the kids? Is there anything we should discuss?

Riva: As a matter of fact, there is, but I didn't know how to bring it up. Alice has started experimenting with cigarettes.

Ray: Alice? Oh, no! She is only 15 years old! How can she be so stupid? I will not tolerate her smoking!

Riva: I don't think she understands how serious it is to begin or how hard it is to stop.

Ray: How could she *not* know? She saw how hard it's been for me.

Riva: Yeah, but kids that age think they will live forever. Remember when you were a kid?

Ray: Sometimes I'd like to forget. (They laugh together.) She must be hanging out with other kids who smoke. That's the only reason she'd be starting so young. That peer pressure stuff is strong. By the way, how do you know she's smoking?

Riva: I drove past the mall the other day and saw her with a cigarette in her mouth.

Ray: That makes it pretty clear. Did you talk to her?

Riva: No, because I was afraid of starting a fight. You know how that goes sometimes.

Ray: (chuckles nervously) Hmmm. How *should* we talk with her? What should we say?

Riva: I think you should be the one to talk to her. She doesn't listen to me.

Ray: You're not alone in that. Every time I say more than 10 words, little flaps come down over her ears and she turns stone deaf.

Riva bursts out laughing. One thing she especially admires in her husband is his good sense of humor. It makes her feel less hopeless about the problem. They walk together in silence for a moment while they think about what to do.

Commentary

These parents are working well together. You may have noticed that they are not following the structured guidelines for sending and receiving, and paraphrasing. These steps aren't always necessary when people are communicating well. They are obviously listening to each other and moving the discussion forward.

The problem the Blenders are facing is a difficult one because it involves peer pressure. Smoking is part of belonging in some peer groups. In other peer groups, there is very little pressure to take up the habit. As adolescents grow older, their peer group exerts more and more influence. It is difficult for parents to help their children choose good, wholesome friends, but this is an important factor in the kinds of activities and attitudes your children are exposed to. It was pointed out in the introduction that the values you promote at home also make an important contribution to your teenager's standards. The studies conducted at Oregon Research Institute have shown that children who smoke tend to come from families with parents who smoke. The Blenders have a head start on the problem because Ray has already quit the habit, which provides a good role model for his children.

Another factor that makes this a difficult issue is that Alice considers smoking to be a matter of personal choice, even though it is bad for her health and she is under the legal age. Alice would view her parents' involvement as extremely intrusive, and she would probably use phrases like "It's my life, and I want you to leave me alone," when her parents confront her about smoking. When you take a position that is not appreciated by adolescents on a sensitive issue, it may help to remember that the strength of their convictions will fade with time. We have even heard young adults say to their parents, "Why didn't you push me harder in school?" when these same individuals fiercely resisted their parents' attempts to help them get better grades when they were in high school. It's like the old cliche about piano lessons, when parents tell their children, "You'll thank me for this some day." The parents have a responsibility to consider the long-term consequences that may result from what their children are or are not doing.

The Blenders, like other families, are not likely to solve this problem quickly. They may be able to keep Alice from smoking, but they can't do it by simply giving her a long lecture, or by making dire threats about grounding her and preventing her from ever being with her friends again. It will take time to come up with a good plan to work on this problem, and Alice will have to agree to cooperate.

Make a list of five or six ways Riva and Ray can start the conversation with Alice about smoking before reading further.

Act VI: The Brainstorming Session

The Scene. Riva and Ray are eating lunch at a restaurant as they discuss how to approach the problem of Alice's smoking.

Ray: Shall we toss a coin to see who records the ideas?
Riva: OK. I'll take heads.

Ray: (tosses the coin) Get out the pad and pencil. You've got the job.

Riva: (She smiles as she takes the pad and pencil.) I guess it's just my lucky day.

Ray: (He sighs as he starts thinking about Alice's smoking problem.) I've been giving this issue a lot of thought since we first talked, and in many ways I feel I'm responsible. I used to be a smoker, so I haven't set a very good example. Secondly, she *is* my daughter.

Riva: (smiling in a friendly way) She sure is.

Ray: So I think I should be the one who presents the issue to her. We should keep you out of this as much as possible.

Riva: (She reaches over and gives his hand a warm squeeze, appreciating the fact that he is being so sensitive to her position with Alice.) Thanks, honey. I really think you're wonderful.

Ray is slightly embarrassed but pleased by his wife's response. He shifts around in his seat and smiles at her. Meanwhile, Riva writes down the idea.

Riva: So you'll talk to her, and I'll try to stay out of it, but what should you say to her?

Ray: I'm not sure.

Riva: We could say we were going to punish her whenever we catch her smoking.

Ray: I like that. But what should the punishment be?

Riva: I don't know; let's come back to that later. I'll put a star next to that idea.

Ray: OK. Another possibility is to reward her for not smoking.

Riva: Or, we could make her smoke herself sick, like you did when you were quitting.

Ray: That's pretty heavy for a kid her age. But write it down. How about giving her some information about how bad cigarettes are for your health?

Riva: (laughing) Sure, but I don't think a long lecture on health would impress her. You could also remind her that it's against the law for children her age to smoke.

Ray: We both know that wouldn't do much good. I can just imagine how I would look standing on a soapbox looking serious and waving my arms around.

Riva: Yes, and I can just see Alice, slumped down in her chair, pouting, tapping her foot impatiently. (They chuckle over this image of Ray and Alice.) I have an idea! We could make her write an essay on the effects of smoking on the body.

Ray: Great idea! We could even use the essay as a punishment. Every time she gets caught smoking, she would have to write another essay.

Riva: Let's make it be 10 pages long!

Ray: Do they have groups for kids, like Smokers Anonymous, that we could send her to?

Riva: I've never heard of anything like that, but it would be nice. I'll write it down and we can check it out.

They order another cup of coffee and decide to have a piece of pie before they begin evaluating their ideas. Here is the list of their ideas:

1. Ray presents the issue to Alice.
2. Riva stays out of it.
3. Punish smoking.
4. Reward not smoking.
5. Have Alice smoke herself sick.
6. Give her information about the bad effects of smoking.
7. Lecture her from a soapbox.
8. Make her write an essay as punishment for smoking.
9. Send her to a group like Smokers Anonymous.

Commentary

That brainstorming session was fairly easy because the parents were united, and no one was defensive or angry. They did start to evaluate some of their options, however, before it was time to do this. This is a common mistake. But they managed to get back on track by simply reminding one another not to evaluate the solutions until later.

Act VII: A Plan in the Making

The Scene. Riva and Ray are sitting in the living room as they begin the process of evaluating each of the options on their list. The children are not home. Riva and Ray begin by looking for options that they both think should be eliminated. They decide to forget about #5 because they thought it might be harmful, #7 because it was silly, and #9 because they didn't know of any such group. Next, they decided to combine #1 and #2 as part of their general strategy. They agreed that Ray would monitor the problem, and he would be responsible for handling the discussions with Alice. Riva would stay away from the firing line. That left items #3, #4, #6, and #8 to consider. Let's listen in as Riva and Ray discuss these options.

Riva: What are the pros and cons of punishing smoking?

Ray: Well, one drawback is that we, or at least I, would probably be involved in a lot of confrontations with her.

Riva: That's true. But an advantage is that I would probably have less.

Ray: Hmmm. That may be true. Another disadvantage is that it would be hard to monitor Alice's smoking. How do we know when she's smoking?

Riva: We would have to check on her closely for a while.

Ray: How would we do that?

Riva: We would have to look for signs of smoking. Actually, you would have to do that, since you're in charge.

Ray: What would I have to do?

Riva: You would have to notice whether her breath and her clothes smell like smoke. You would also have to look in her purse to see if she is carrying cigarettes or matches, and go in her room every now and then to find out if she has been smoking in there.

Ray: Wouldn't that be an invasion of privacy?

Riva: Maybe so. But it is one way we can steer her away from a bad habit. If we want her to stop smoking, we are going to have to pay attention to her for a while.

Ray: In a sense, giving her more attention would be an advantage and a disadvantage at the same time. It would probably be better for all of us if I was a little more involved in her life. I don't give her much attention.

Riva: That's true, but you are always working so hard.

Ray: Sometimes I wonder about my priorities, though. Of course work is important, but so is our family.

Riva: So you would be more involved. (She writes that down as an advantage.) What's another advantage of using punishment? I can't think of any. I hate to punish the kids, even though I seem to be doing it all the time. Maybe that's why it's so unpleasant for me.

Ray: I hate it, too. But it works when we are consistent about it.

Riva: Yeah, *if* we're consistent.

Ray: OK, OK. We both need to be more consistent, but let's move on. What's good and bad about rewarding her for not smoking?

Riva: It's easy to think of some disadvantages to that. What if we reward her because we think she isn't smoking, but she is just being sneaky?

Ray: (He's slightly irritated by this comment because it reveals Riva's negative slant toward his daughter, but he bites his lip and remains neutral.) That's always a possibility, but if I am more involved and monitor her carefully it shouldn't be a big problem. Even if we make a mistake every now and then, I think it would help the program seem less severe.

Riva: I think so, too. You know, she really cares about you. Maybe she would want to give up cigarettes if she thought it would make you happy.

Ray: I wish it were that easy! (He looks at the next idea on the list.) I really like this one: "Give her information." Where can we get some pamphlets on the effects of smoking?

Riva: I can call the counselor at Alice's school and ask for some suggestions. Or, maybe I should try the county public health department. They must have some information.

Ray: I'll bet the public library would have something, too. And what about the American Cancer Society, or that community referral service? Wouldn't they know?

Riva: Good idea! Also, there are several drug counseling services. And maybe I'll give the pediatrician's office a call too while I'm at it. They always have pamphlets.

Ray: If we had some pamphlets around the house, Alice would see them and so would the other kids.

Riva: One thing I like about using pamphlets as a source of information is that we don't have to do the lecture routine.

Ray: Right. The information comes from the experts.

Riva: The only disadvantage I can see with this idea is the effort involved in getting the information.

Commentary

During the process of evaluating solutions, these parents are getting into another level of brainstorming. As they consider each idea, they think about the steps required to carry it out. This refining process is needed and appropriate at this stage. It is when you visualize *how* a proposed solution would work that you begin to notice what you have to *do* to make it work. Make sure you spell out these details now because you will need them when you write up the final agreement.

Ray: Will you look for the pamphlets since I am the one who has to deal with her directly?

Riva: Sure. All that is involved is some telephone work. It's the least I can do to help.

Ray: Thanks. And while you do that, maybe you could check on whether there is a Smokers Anonymous group.

Riva: OK. But let's consider this next idea. It's my favorite.

Ray: Which one is that?

Riva: Writing an essay each time you catch her smoking.

Ray: What do you like about it?

Riva: It will make her think more carefully about what she is doing to her body, and it gives her writing skills a boost.

Ray: That's all very well and good, but how do you make her do it? You know it's not going to be easy.

Riva: We could ground her until it's done.

Ray: I thought we were trying to stay away from grounding.

Riva: That's true. But in this case, the grounding is over as soon as she finishes the essay.

Ray: What if she does a rotten job on the paper?

Riva: Make her do it again until it's satisfactory.

Ray: That seems hard to do to me.

Riva: So we should put that down as a disadvantage. It would be hard to do.

Ray: I'm beginning to like the idea, but 10 pages is pretty long.

Riva: Let's shorten it, then.

Ray: That's reasonable. How about two pages?

Riva: That sounds good to me.

Commentary

Now these parents are in a good position to decide on a course of action that is agreeable to both of them. The options they are considering are actually a combination of several of the ideas that were generated during their brainstorming session. Here is their list of pros and cons. Let's see how they use it.

Punish Alice for Smoking
(Ray is responsible for this.)

Pros	*Cons*
1. Monitoring means increased involvement for Ray.	1. Ray has more confrontations with Alice.
2. Consistent punishment works.	2. Smoking is hard to monitor.

Reward Alice for Not Smoking

Pros	*Cons*
1. Positive attention might make Alice more cooperative.	1. Alice might be rewarded for lying.
2. Alice might stop smoking if she thought it would make Ray happy.	

Give Alice Information about the Effects of Smoking
(Riva will pick up some pamphlets.)

Pros	*Cons*
1. All the children will see the pamphlets.	1. It takes effort to find the information.
2. The advice comes from the experts, not from us.	
3. We don't have to argue about it.	

Have Alice Write a Two-Page Essay

Pros	*Cons*
1. It will make Alice think about what she is doing to her body.	1. Have to check it.
2. Gives Alice's writing skills a boost.	2. Hard to make Alice do it over until it's satisfactory.
	3. Have to ground Alice until the essay is done.

Ray: So, looking over this list, is there anything you would like to eliminate?

Riva: The rewards.

Ray: Anything else?

Riva: No.

Ray: Well, that's the one that I like. Since we don't agree, I guess we should leave it on the list. I would like to eliminate the essay, but I guess you like that one.

Riva: Right.

Ray: So we can't eliminate anything. Let's look at it another way. What are your favorite ideas?

Riva: I like "giving information" and the "essay."

Ray: I agree with you on information. I like rewards and punishment, too.

Riva: How about if we agree to follow through on the information idea? I'll get some pamphlets and leave them around the house in places where they can't be missed.

Ray: Like the bathroom.

Riva: (smiling) Yeah. That seems to be a popular reading spot.

Ray: And after they've been around for a while, you and I could talk about what we read in the pamphlet when the kids are around.

Riva: OK, that sounds good. But I think we need more ammunition for this problem. Don't you?

Ray: Yes. Punishing her seems like a good idea, too.

Riva: (nodding her head) Uh-huh.

Ray: I could monitor her regularly, like you suggested. That would mean that I would have to check her breath and clothes and look in her purse. Isn't there any way I could do this without being a private investigator?

Riva: That's hard. I speak from experience.

Ray: Yeah. I hadn't thought of it that way before.

Riva: Should we brainstorm about that?

Ray: OK, but let's do it another time. I'm getting tired.

Riva: Me, too. This has been a lot of work.

Ray: Yes, it has. But you know, I feel good about our new approach. I think we have a much better chance of turning Alice away from smoking by working together. Anything has got to be better than the screaming fights we used to have with her about things like this.

Riva: You can say that again.

Ray: Let's write down what we have decided so far, and then let's go to a movie. We've earned it.

Commentary

It is important not to take on too much at one time. It may take several sessions to come up with a workable approach to a difficult problem. Ray and Riva have made enormous progress on this sensitive issue. They can refine their approach later when they have more energy and some fresh ideas. In the meantime, they can begin their campaign by getting some pamphlets and leaving them around the house. They can also use their list of options and the notes from this last session as a starting place for their next discussion.

Here is what Ray and Riva's agreement looks like:

May 29, 2004

Beginning Strategies to Stop Alice's Smoking

1. Ray will take charge of the discussions and confrontations with Alice about cigarette smoking.
2. Riva will not be directly involved in dealing with Alice on this issue.
3. Riva will get some pamphlets on the effects of cigarette smoking on health. She will make several calls around the community to find out where these pamphlets are available.
4. Ray and Riva will leave the pamphlets in strategic locations around the house.
5. Ray will bring up the topic of the effects of smoking on health at a good time when the children are present. The discussion will not be directed toward Alice or anyone else. It will be a general discussion. Riva will help.
6. Ray and Riva will meet to brainstorm punishments and rewards next week on Friday night, over dinner at the restaurant of Riva's choice.

Riva and Ray

Now let's consider another example of managing sensitive issues as the Wrights try to deal with a problem that every father can identify with.

The Family Tools

Craig borrows his father's tools, which is permitted, but he frequently forgets to return them to their appropriate places, and this *is* a problem. Dad becomes very irritated when this happens, because he is careful with his tools. He likes to be able to go to his toolbox and find what he needs quickly. When something is missing, he often explodes and everyone in the household runs for cover. Even Dad is surprised at how angry he gets.

Act I: Soothing the Tempest

The Scene. Dad and Craig have just had another yelling confrontation. It took 20 minutes for Dad to find his handsaw because Craig left it outside in the rain and it rusted. This time Mom intervenes because it looks as if they are on the verge of a physical confrontation. Mom makes the two of them agree to talk about it later. She sends Craig outside to finish his chores in the yard, and she suggests to Dad that he work off some steam on his exercise bike. Kathy knows that exercising will make Dad feel better. Then maybe they can talk calmly about this situation.

Kathy makes fresh coffee while John finishes his shower. The discussion begins after they are seated comfortably in the living room.

Kathy: I'm sorry you and Craig had another fight about the tools.

John: (Misunderstanding her intent, he assumes she is going to accuse him of being unreasonable.) I hope you're not going to tell me that I'm being too hard on Craig.

Kathy: (in a soothing tone of voice) No, Craig needs to learn to put your tools back where they belong.

John: That's right! I'm glad *you* understand what I'm trying to tell him.

Kathy: The question is, how can we teach him? There's got to be a way. We just have to put our minds to it.

John: Well, I've told him in every way I know. He has to return my goddamned tools to their proper place! I don't know how I can communicate the message any more clearly.

Kathy: Maybe the way to do it is not with words.

John: Well, what do you suggest?

Kathy: Teach him with actions.

John: (smiling) You mean, action speaks louder than words?

Kathy: (smiling back) I'll bet we can think of something that would work if we give it a good try.

John: How should we begin?

Kathy: I think the first step is to gather information for a few days and then come back and talk about it again.

John: OK, that sounds good. I'll talk to some of my friends to see how they handle it. (He gives Kathy a hug, and they smile at each other.)

Commentary

It takes a high order of skill to soothe negative emotions, and Kathy did this very well. At each stage, her response cooled down an otherwise hot situation. She did this by staying calm herself and acting in a caring way. John Gottman, who has studied marital conflict for nearly four decades, first pointed out the importance of soothing. He concluded from his observations of couples that there are certain moments during intimate conversations when *soothing* can change conflict into an opportunity to change. It took maturity for Kathy to intervene with gentle concern and understanding. Since she was not involved, Kathy was in a good position to provide support. This made it possible for the parents to work *together* instead of being at odds with each other. The parent who is not under fire can support the other. This is an advantage two-parent families have that is sorely missed in single-parent homes.

The soothing began when Kathy redirected the intense negative energy that was building up as Craig and Dad were arguing about the tools. Her strategy was to separate them by sending Craig outside to do physical labor and convincing Dad to exercise. She did this by talking calmly to each of them. Notice that Kathy did not treat them equally, although she felt as though she should because they were both out of control. She treated Craig like a child (which he is) and her husband like a partner (which he is). Kathy was firm with Craig when she gave him the direct command, "Craig, go outside now and finish your yard work. You're almost done." As soon as Craig left the scene, she gently suggested to John that he would feel better if he burned off some steam on his bike. Kathy's intervention was successful because she was not angry and there was no edge in her voice as she delivered her messages. In this way, she managed to cool off an otherwise hot situation.

Creating some "space" was a key element for improving the situation. This included separating the warriors, changing their activities, and letting some time pass before attempting to deal with the problem. *Trying to solve problems when people are upset does not work.*

Physical exercise releases endorphins into your bloodstream, which make you feel good. Endorphins are nature's own high. For this reason, having both Dad and Craig engage in physical activities was a particularly good ploy.

When Kathy and John were finally alone together in the living room and John was feeling more cheerful, Kathy approached the topic in a soothing manner. Even though John initially misinterpreted her intentions, Kathy responded with understanding rather than irritability. An irritable reaction at this point would have sent John into a tirade about his tools. She knew from past experience that John simply wanted Craig to put the tools away, and she expressed that in a straightforward manner. This made John feel she understood the problem. The tools had been an issue between father and son for a long time, so Kathy suggested moving slowly. Then the two adults agreed to work together on resolving this sensitive issue.

If you don't have a partner to share in your parenting, draw on the support of friends. It's difficult to solve problems on your own, and other people can give you new perspectives and insights. They can also calm you down and help you see the brighter side of the picture. When you are involved in a problem, it is very difficult to be objective about it. That's just one reason why good friends are so valuable.

Asking "Why?"

It is often tempting to introduce a problem to adolescents by asking *why* they are doing something that causes problems for others. This does not change behavior, but most parents go through this step anyway. People don't know the real reasons for their behavior. We may think we know, but we are just kidding ourselves. We rationalize our behavior by making up stories about the events that have taken place. *Unfortunately, these stories are seldom grounded in reality.* In fact, these reasons "why" we do things can interfere with the process of changing behavior because the stories people tell themselves tend to sidetrack the issue. So don't bother asking your teenager why. It is better to ask *how* the problem can be solved. Here's what happened when Dad asked Craig to tell him why he doesn't put the tools back. Notice that Dad started out calmly, but the exchange heated up quickly.

Act II: Tell Me Why

The Scene. Dad and Craig are sitting in the living room, and Dad decides to bring up the issue of the tools.

Dad: Why don't you put my tools away?

Craig: I don't put them back because I forget.

Dad: Why do you forget?

Craig: Because I have so many other things on my mind. Something comes up and I just forget. I don't do it to bug you. You know, I don't *enjoy* having you yell at me.

Dad: (John can feel himself getting irritated all over again because he knows that he has a lot more on his mind than his 15-year-old son, who seems to do nothing but go to school and talk on the telephone. He raises his voice and makes a terse statement.) And I don't *enjoy* having my tools left out in the rain, either!

Craig: (sighing loudly and rolling his eyes) It's impossible to talk to you about anything. (He gets up and leaves the room.)

Commentary

Clearly, this exchange did not help to resolve the issue, and Dad and Craig both came away feeling as though the situation is hopeless.

After this futile attempt to talk to Craig about the issue, John decided that he needed some new ideas. Friends can be a great resource if you know how to exchange information. Let's look in as John asks his good friend, Will, for some advice.

Act III: A Glimmer of Hope

The Scene. John and Will are having a coffee break in the cafeteria at work. They both have workshops at home, and they enjoy talking about their various projects. Will has been making an entertainment center for his TV and stereo, and the two men have been discussing some of the design problems.

John: How are you doing on your project?

Will: I'm almost done. Your ideas really helped.

John: Thanks. You know, thinking about the best way to do a project is the fun part; it's doing it that's hard. Especially when you can't find your tools. That reminds me, I could use some ideas on where to trade in that son of mine.

Will: Oh, come on—Craig is a great kid! What happened?

John: I can't get Craig to return my tools, and it makes me furious! I found my good handsaw out in the yard where Craig had left it for two weeks. It was so rusted that I had to go out and buy a new one. I was so mad at Craig, I just about lost it with him. It's a good thing Kathy was there to keep things under control.

Will: It's funny how something like that can really make a person upset with their kids. But I know what you mean. I would really be angry if my son did that to one of my tools.

John: Part of it is that I want Craig to learn about being responsible with tools, especially when he borrows them. The other part is that I only have so much time to work on projects at home, and if I have to spend 30 minutes looking for my tools, I don't even feel like getting started.

Will: I agree with you on that. But Craig is only 15. You still have some time left before you should give up on him. Kids that age go around with their heads in a fog. My kids were pretty flaky at that age.

John: Well, you're right about that. Craig is a regular fog machine! You'd think a smart kid like that could learn a simple rule: Put the tools where they belong.

Will: But Craig has his saving graces. He's certainly competent with a boat on the river. I haven't seen many kids—or even men—who can handle a boat like your boy.

John: Well, that's true.

Will: And when I've hired him to work on my yard, he's been polite, and he does a thorough job.

John: Does he put the yard tools away at your house?

Will: As a matter of fact, he does. But then kids are on their best behavior when they are at somebody else's house. People are always telling us how charming *our* kids are. That's news to me!

John: That's another thing that makes me mad. Why can't our kids treat us with the same respect they do their friends—or perfect strangers, for that matter? After all, *we're* the ones who give them everything!

Commentary

One of the great things about good friends is that they listen to your troubles sympathetically. It really helps to be able to unload your problems on someone every once in a while. All too often, family members don't want to hear your story because they are involved in it or they have heard it a dozen times already.

Another way friends help out in situations like this is to put things in a positive framework. Will did this several times for John. First, he reassured John that Craig was really no different from other teenagers, who also have a tendency to conveniently "forget" about their responsibilities. Second, Will helped to change John's perspective about Craig by mentioning some of the things that he really admires, such as Craig's competence in handling a boat, his politeness, and his thoroughness when he works in Will's yard. This points out one of the surprising characteristics of teenagers. They can be absolutely unbearable with their own family and perfectly charming when they are around other people. This is actually a good sign because it means that your adolescent does know how to behave appropriately.

Act IV: Hammurabi's Tools

The Scene. John and Kathy are sitting in the living room. The conversation begins as they share the information they have gathered from talking to other people about the issue.

Kathy: Well, John, you are not alone in your problem with tools. I have also noticed that Jody forgets to return *my* tools.

John: What tools do you have?

Kathy: Women's tools. They aren't hammers and screwdrivers, but that doesn't mean they aren't tools.

John: (laughing) Tell me about your problems. Maybe they'll help me forget mine.

Kathy: I have noticed that my beauty tools have a way of disappearing. At my age I need the best equipment to look good—things like fancy hair conditioners, moisturizing creams, and all that expensive stuff. I, too, suffer when I look for my tools and they are missing.

John: You poor thing. This could be serious! (They laugh about this together, which puts them both in a better mood.)

Kathy: I was in the shower yesterday washing my hair when I noticed that my conditioner was missing. I had to get out of the shower, wrap myself in a towel, and drip my way through the house to the kids' bathroom to collect *my* conditioner! I was so mad at Jody that I would have really chewed her out if she had been around. When I thought about the situation with Craig and your tools I understood why it makes you so mad when he doesn't put them away.

John: (He finds this really amusing. Hearing his wife express the same kinds of feelings helps him to disengage from his problem with Craig.) So what can we do about the kids not returning our stuff? There must be some way to deal with it other than sending them to a foster home until they are 25.

Kathy: Actually, I do have an idea!

John: You have my undivided attention.

Kathy: I was talking about our problem with my friend Kate, and she said she sometimes has the same problem with her daughter, Brooke. But she figured out a little trick that really seems to work for her. Whenever something of hers is missing, she takes something of Brooke's.

John: You mean Hammurabi's old law of "an eye for an eye and a tooth for a tooth"? Isn't that kind of primitive?

Kathy: Well, Hammurabi's law applied to body parts, but in this case it makes sense, partly because the punishment is so small. For example, Kate once took Brooke's telephone out of her room and hid it. Brooke was frantically looking all over the house for it. Kate calmly told her that she had it, and she would be glad to return it as soon as her pink blouse was returned, washed and ironed, to her closet.

John: That's great! I like that! What could I take of Craig's?

Kathy: What does he use on a daily basis that he absolutely can't live without?

John: Hmmm. Let's see. Maybe his bike . . .

Commentary

That was a good example of a couple resolving a sensitive issue by working together. It's what most of us thought married life would be like—sharing good times and working as a team to raise children and overcome difficulties.

Notice how humor enhanced the discussion. Also, John and Kathy used one another's perspective to expand the way each of them felt about the issue. Notice that gathering information by asking friends for advice was an important resource for solving the problem. Now they have a plan for managing the problem. The next step is to introduce the issue at a family meeting and tell the children about the new consequences for borrowing something and not returning it.

Key Ideas in This Chapter

1. Decide in advance *what* the problem is, *who* to present it to, and *when, where,* and *how* to introduce it.
2. Practice your opening statements.
3. Remove all negative words, gestures, tones, and feelings from your introduction.
4. Focus on a simple, single goal—make it a statement of what you would like in the future. Write it down so you won't forget it.
5. Present the problem in a positive light.
6. Solicit the assistance of friends and/or family members.
7. Make the introduction short and to the point.
8. Use humor.
9. Be prepared to soothe the other person's feelings.
10. Minimize the problem. This makes it easier for people to believe that change is possible.
11. Be understanding. Try to see the problem from the other person's perspective.

12. Take your time. You won't solve most problems right away. The more complex they are and the longer they've been around, the stronger the feelings about them and the more challenging they will be to resolve.

Chapter Five Homework Assignment

1. From the list of issues you have been collecting, select a problem that has been difficult for your family to talk about. Discuss the issue with one or two friends, and observe how they address the problem. Does one person seem more negative than another? Did one friend seem to help you think more clearly about the issue?
2. Take notes for a few days on how the family responds to the issue. Try to see the issue from other people's perspectives.
3. Look for some humorous aspects to the problem, especially with regard to your own behavior.
4. Design two introduction strategies. One should be designed to elicit a negative response from family members. The other should be designed to create a positive, cooperative feeling. Practice the two introductions in front of a mirror.
5. Approach the issue in small steps. During the next family forum simply present and receive information about the issue, then try changing roles. If the discussion doesn't become too heated, go on to the brainstorming stage. Post the list of options on the refrigerator for two or three days before you attempt to evaluate solutions. Then go over the suggestions and narrow down the list. Finally, try to write up an agreement; it may take several meetings to accomplish this end result.

Guidelines for Good Introductions

1. Plan ahead.
2. Ask yourself the following questions:
   a. *When* is the best time to bring up the issue?
   b. *Who* is the best person to talk with first?

     c. *Where* should you introduce the problem?

     d. *What* should you say?

3. Consult with friends.
4. If you can, engage a neutral family member as a consultant.
5. Practice your presentation.
6. Be pleasant and calm.
7. Have a single, simple goal in mind.
8. Accept some responsibility for the issue.

SECTION II

Introduction

The chapters in this section apply the problem-solving skills and techniques for regulating emotions that you learned in Section I to three sensitive topics that concern parents of adolescents: teaching sexual responsibility, controlling drug use, and fostering academic achievement.

This section pulls together bits and pieces from *Part 1: The Basics* and the first section of this book as we negotiate and problem solve our way through the adolescent briar patch. Getting a few scratches along the way is unavoidable, but by now you should have a good set of tools to help you handle almost any situation. Sometimes issues are addressed in the family forum, and at other times the highly structured approach outlined in the first section of this book is not rigorously followed.

Even though we have attempted to present as much information as possible, it should be acknowledged that entire books have been written on topics such as communication, drugs and alcohol, sexual issues, and so on. There are many other components that can be added to what you have learned here. Seek out other resources, and carefully observe what is going on in your family.

By the time you finish this book, you should feel that it is possible to plan the way you live together as a family. Making some mistakes along the way is unavoidable. But your children will forgive you, just as you will forgive them for their mistakes. As long as your family takes tiny steps that lead in the right direction, your children can become happy, productive members of society.

CHAPTER 6

The Sexual Adolescent

The Adolescent Myth

For some reason, adolescents seldom entertain the idea that their parents are sexual beings. If they think about it at all, they assume that once, long ago in a place far away, their mothers and fathers had a sexual encounter. This exchange produced the divine product (them), and then the reproductive apparatus withered away and sexual desire conveniently disappeared. The underlying assumption is that parents are celibate beings with only ancient memories of sex to help them guide their children. This explains why adolescents are often surprised when their parents are audacious enough to offer advice or, heaven forbid, to set limits on their sexual activities.

Teaching the Basics

It is important for children to learn about sexuality in a matter-of-fact way from caring parents who provide age-appropriate information. Parents usually begin teaching their children about the

137

human body during the preschool years. At this stage, the facts about the sexual organs are included but not emphasized; most small children know that boys have a penis and girls have a vagina. As children mature, it is appropriate to give them increasingly specific details about sexuality. Many adults are reluctant or embarrassed to talk about these matters, however, and this discomfort is communicated nonverbally. When adults talk about sex they may blush, fail to maintain good eye contact, or laugh nervously. This manner of presentation by adults makes it difficult for children to accept sex as a natural part of adult life. All too often, children's first lessons about sex have negative overtones, even though their parents didn't mean for it to be that way.

If parents fail to provide proper guidance, children learn about sex in an unplanned way from their peers or the media. The forbidden nature of the topic makes it alluring, and by the time children reach their early teens their classmates are preoccupied with the subject. The problem with learning about sex from peers is that the information is often distorted or inappropriate. Movies and television also contribute to the misconceptions children have about sexuality. The sensational aspects of sex tend to be emphasized in prime-time programming, and the seedy side is graphically presented in "soaps" and talk shows. Perhaps worst of all, Hollywood seems to promote an association between sex and violence in horror films, which, unfortunately, are popular with teenagers.

By the time children are in high school, they have a basic understanding of the rituals of courtship and the mechanics of sex, but there are many gaps in their knowledge of other related issues such as sexually transmitted diseases and contraceptives. Many parents assume that their adolescents are learning about these issues in sex-education classes at school but this varies from one school district to another. This means it is up to parents to make sure their children are adequately prepared before they become sexually active as young adults.

Parents tend to be intimidated by the prospect of discussing sex with their teenagers. If you want to talk to your adolescent about sex but are uncomfortable about it, plan ahead and practice first.

There are several ways to do this. A spouse or good friend can help you rehearse your presentation by role-playing with you. You can also practice out loud in front of a mirror, or record your speech and play it back. If all of these approaches make you uneasy, then just picture the conversation in your mind. Think about your adolescent's level of understanding, and imagine that he or she is sitting in front of you listening to what you are saying. Try to anticipate how your adolescent will respond and the questions he or she might ask. The goal is to make your discussion about sex seem relatively simple and straightforward. Whatever you do, don't avoid the issue altogether and hope that your teenager will learn from others. Such sources are seldom reliable and may not represent your set of values. It is all right to feel awkward or uncomfortable as long as it does not prevent you from carrying out this important parental responsibility.

The topic of sex should be presented in a positive light, regardless of your position on sexual matters. If you believe sex is only for procreation, then think of the miracle that makes it possible for two humans to create a new life. If you think sex is a good way for two people to express their joy and love for one another, then try to communicate this. Let your children know that sex is not a bad or frightening experience when you are an adult.

If you dislike intercourse yourself or feel certain that you cannot discuss it with your youngsters, then find some other adult you can trust (a friend, a minister, or a counselor), and ask that person to help. If your children indicate they already know about sex, don't take this to mean that your responsibility is over. You can still have a positive influence by sharing information and expressing your values. It's never too late. An honest discussion will help them appreciate the fact that sex is a pleasant, but serious, adult experience they are not quite ready for. Acknowledge that kissing and holding hands are activities that young adolescents can experiment with. Teach them about caring for another person in a relationship, and discuss what that means. Sex is more than the act itself, although teenagers and parents tend to forget this at times.

Act I: Martha Learns about Menstruation

The Scene. Betty is the mother in this family, and she has raised her two children more or less on her own. She and her husband were divorced when the children were still toddlers. Her daughter, Martha, is now 10 years old and her son, Ricky, just turned 9 last month. Mom explains menstruation to Martha while they unload groceries in the kitchen.

Martha: (holding up a box of tampons) What are these for, Mom? I know you use them for your period, but I don't really know what that is either. Doesn't it have something to do with making babies?

Mom: Those are tampons, and I use them when I have a period. And, yes, it does have something to do with making babies. Most women menstruate about once a month.

Martha: Mens . . . what?

Mom: (laughing) M-e-n-s-t-r-u-a-t-e (She spells it out.) That's the same as having a period—it means that there is some blood that comes out of the vagina.

Martha: Why do women bleed like that?

Mom: Well, it's a long story. Are you sure you want to hear about it now?

Martha: I'd like to know, and I've got nothing else to do while I help you put this stuff away.

Mom: (She continues to put the fresh vegetables away in the refrigerator.) Every month, a woman's body releases an egg that is ready to be fertilized by the sperm that comes out of a man's penis during sex. If the egg is fertilized, it becomes attached to the wall of the uterus. Do you know where your uterus is?

Martha: I think so. (She points to her vagina.)

Mom: Well, that's close. It's just below your belly button. I'll show you later in a book. Anyway, the fertilized egg stays in the uterus and grows into a baby. If the egg isn't fertilized, which is most of the time, then it passes through the body without becoming attached to the uterus.

Martha: But why does that make you bleed?

Mom: Because each month the uterus prepares a thick lining with nourishing blood to get ready in case the egg is fertilized. If the egg isn't fertilized, it is discharged from the body along with the extra blood that has been saved up in the lining of the uterus. The blood and the egg leave the body through your vagina. Tampons are used by women to absorb the blood and keep it from getting all over their clothes.

Martha: Yuk. That sounds terrible. Does it hurt?

Mom: Sometimes it hurts a little. But not as much as you might think, when you see all that blood. Mostly it's just messy. I usually don't wear white pants when I'm menstruating, for example, because tampons don't always work perfectly.

Martha: That's gross! Is that going to happen to me? Will I start bleeding down there, too?

Mom: Yes, some day you will. But it isn't bad. It's just part of being able to have babies, which is one of the wonderful things about being a woman. Sometime in the next couple of years you will have your first period. When that happens, it means you are becoming a young woman.

Martha: When I start bleeding, does it mean I can get pregnant?

Mom: You probably could, but having babies at an early age is hard on both the mother and the baby. Your body will continue to grow and develop until you're at least 18 years old, or even into your early 20s. If your body is trying to nourish a baby while you are still growing, it can interfere with your own development. And besides, you need to have a father who is old enough to help you raise the baby and support the family. But for some reason, our bodies start menstruating before we're ready to have babies. Now go put the toothpaste away in the bathroom.

Martha: But, Mom, I want to know more about this. How soon will I start? Will it happen when I'm 13 or 14?

Mom: It starts at a different time for each person. I started when I was 14. My sister started when she was 12. You'll probably start to develop breasts first, and then you'll have your first period. At least that's the way it usually happens.

Martha: Well, I've started to get breasts—haven't you noticed?

Mom: (holding back a smile, because she hadn't noticed anything yet) No, I don't think I've noticed it yet, but you may be right. The first sign that your breasts are growing is that they get a little sensitive or sore. And sometimes just before your period, you'll notice your breasts getting a bit sore. By the way, if you spot in your panties, come and tell me.

Martha: What do you mean, spot?

Mom: For some girls, drops of blood will show up in their panties just before they start having a real period. Other girls just start bleeding full force.

Martha: Can you bleed to death from this?

Mom: No, sweetie. It's perfectly normal to bleed from your vagina when you have your period, and it's really only a little bit of blood. Now go and put the toothpaste away.

Commentary

Menstruation and breast development are two of the most noticeable changes for young girls, and Mom answered her daughter's questions about these areas of concern without adding unnecessary details. Mom also did a good job of presenting menstruation as a normal part of being a woman. By sharing some details about her own growth and development, Mom made it easier for Martha to talk to her about the changes she may notice in her body.

Boys also need to know what to expect as their bodies begin to change during puberty. Among other things, these changes signal the beginning of involuntary erections and nocturnal emissions, or wet dreams. Boys should be told that this is perfectly normal, even though it can be embarrassing when it occurs. It may be helpful to explain some of the physical changes they are going through and to let them know that you are willing to answer their questions. If you aren't sure that you are adequately prepared, ask your pediatrician to fill in the details.

Keep in mind that it becomes easier to talk about these issues with your children after your first discussion. Make it clear that you will try to answer their questions about sex in a matter-of-fact way. Avoid reading intentions into their questions by making statements like, "And why are you interested in this—is that new boyfriend of yours doing something that I should know about?" This will teach your children not to come to you for information, which could have dire consequences.

As you provide basic information about sex, you should also discuss some of the accompanying feelings and thoughts. Perhaps you didn't have strong sexual fantasies or urges when you were an adolescent, but most youngsters do, and it is helpful for parents to openly acknowledge this. Otherwise, your children may think their feelings are unusual, when in reality they are quite normal.

Act II: Martha's Education Continues

Several years have passed since we have looked in on Betty and her family. Martha is now 15 years old, and her sexual development has progressed to a new stage. Last year she started menstruating. During the past five years, Betty has talked with Martha on several occasions about what it's like to have a period. Betty was consistent about checking every now and then to see if Martha had any questions about her body. Martha was looking forward to becoming a woman. Her mother had taught her how to use pads and how to dispose of them properly. They discussed the problem of tampons and the rare but very serious toxic shock syndrome. When Martha had her first period, she and her mother went out to dinner together to celebrate the occasion.

Ricky is almost 14 years old, and he is getting taller every day. Betty realizes that puberty is just around the corner, and she is already behind schedule in talking to him about sex. It had been hard enough for Betty to talk to her daughter—how on earth will she discuss this with her son?

One of Betty's friends mentioned that she used books to teach her children about sex. In some ways, she liked that solution. But, after thinking about it for a while, Betty decided that she wanted to talk directly with her children about sex. She began preparing for this by going to the library and talking to the librarian in the children's section. Since she wanted to talk to her children about sex herself, Betty planned to become knowledgeable on the topic first. The librarian had given her several books to look over. Some of them were written for children, and some of them were for parents. After reviewing these materials, one thing seemed clear—sex education is a complicated topic that has to be dealt with gradually as children develop. There is more to it than simply describing the features of male and female bodies, and explaining reproduction. It is important for children to understand at many different levels the moral issues involved in engaging in intercourse and having babies; and they need to learn basic relationship skills. In order to form a good relationship with someone of the opposite sex, you have to know how to make a commitment and be able to show that you care. Parents play an essential role in determining how their children learn these lessons. Betty also realized that parents need to be involved in monitoring the activities of their children and enforcing the rules concerning dating, attending parties, and curfew hours.

The librarian also recommended visiting the local Planned Parenthood office. Betty gave them a call and arranged to have a meeting with one of the counselors. This turned out to be one of the best resources of all. A well-informed young woman answered Betty's questions in a straightforward and direct manner, and she pulled out books and pamphlets for Betty to look over. The counselor explained that Betty could arrange for a professional to speak to a parent group, the PTA, or a group of youngsters and parents; she also offered several other options. Betty felt much more confident about discussing the topic now that she was armed with all of this new information.

The Scene. The following conversation takes place during summer vacation. The family is in the car on their way to visit relatives who live 60 miles away. Betty and Martha have been hassling with each other about Martha's early curfew. When the discussion takes a sudden turn, Betty capitalizes on the opportunity to give a morality lesson that she feels is overdue. Betty has been dreading this conversation, but she knows there is no way to avoid it.

Martha: I think the reason you want me to come home early is because all you have on your mind is sex. You think that if I'm out after midnight I must be screwing someone.

Mom: Martha, watch your mouth. And, no, I don't think that you just want to stay out late so you can experiment with sex. Frankly, I don't think you are the kind of girl who would get sexually involved with just anyone, and you don't seem to have a steady boyfriend yet.

Ricky starts to giggle in the backseat, and he begins to poke his sister and make faces. Martha responds in kind, and they have a tickling match. Betty uses the break in the conversation to think of a good way to carry on this subject in a lighter vein.

Mom: Calm down, you guys. You're supposed to be teenagers, not preschoolers, so start acting like it. And, yes, I guess I do worry when you are out with boys. Unless things have really changed from the time when I was a teenager . . . (Both kids start snickering and poking each other again.) Yes, I know, I was a teenager back in prehistoric times before fire, the wheel, and sex were invented. But I still remember that there was a lot of pressure from other teenagers to experiment with sex. And it was always the boys who wanted to "go all the way." When I was a girl, you had to say no to stay out of trouble.

Martha: Oh, Mom, it's just like I said. All you're worried about is sex. I know how to take care of myself. You act like

I'm an idiot or something. Why don't you just trust me? I know what I'm doing.

Mom: I know you do, and I do trust you, but that doesn't mean that I shouldn't be concerned or involved. There are still some important lessons for you to learn, and I want to help you make good choices.

Martha: Maybe so, but at least I should have a little privacy in my life, don't you think? (She shoots an angry look at her brother, who is shaking with laughter.)

Ricky: What's the matter? Do I make you nervous or something?

Martha: Oh, shut up. You don't make me nervous, you make me *sick!* (whining) Mom, make him leave me alone!

Later that week, Betty introduced the topic again. This time she was better prepared because she had thought about the subject at length and had discussed it with her close friend, Ruth. They both agreed that it was important to teach Martha how to say no. In fact, they agreed that there were several steps involved in saying no. They weren't sure how to talk about it, since neither of them had received a similar lecture from their parents. Even when they were experimenting with sex as young girls, they hadn't talked about it much. What you did with your boyfriend was considered to be a private matter, which meant that everyone had to learn by trial and error. But now that they began to work on the problem of how to do it right, they enjoyed their discussion.

Betty's friend Ruth had teenage sons of her own to worry about, so she was able to give Betty some useful insights about teenagers and sex.

Act III: Getting Down to Details

The Scene. Betty and Ruth are sitting at the kitchen table having tea. The topic of their conversation is sex and teenagers.

Ruth: Don't you remember that feeling of urgency when you were necking with a boy in the backseat of a car on a back road somewhere? Whew! If I could only work up a little of that same feeling now!

Betty: (laughing) Well, frankly, I had forgotten what it felt like when I was Martha's age. But I guess you're right. In addition to feeling turned on, I remember feeling kind of put upon. Didn't you? It seemed like whenever you went out with a boy he was always putting the make on you, whether you were interested or not. I hated that.

Ruth: Not me! I was hot-blooded. The only thing that kept me from getting into trouble was the fear of getting pregnant. Now that birth control is so available, what *will* keep kids from too much experimentation?

Betty: What about good old morality? My kids are always telling me that I'm old-fashioned, but it seems to me that all moral values are considered old-fashioned today.

Ruth: Well, I don't think so. It's always been like this. Don't you remember your parents saying the same things to you? And don't you remember telling them that their values were old-fashioned?

Betty: OK, OK. But what am I going to say to Martha about sex? What do you think I should tell her?

Ruth: Tell her that sex is something to share with someone she truly loves. It shouldn't be just a cheap thrill to share with every Tom, Dick, and Harry.

Betty: But you know how impressionable teenagers are. They fall in love with someone new every couple of weeks. It all depends on the phase of the moon or who they sit next to in class. If I tell her that, then every time her latest love gets excited and says the right words, she'll be easy prey. It's not a good idea to make it with half of the football team.

Ruth: Well, maybe not *half* of the football team—she needs to save some energy for the basketball team.

They enjoy a good laugh. Then Ruth gets up to make more tea. Betty brings over their dirty dishes, and they tidy up the kitchen together.

Betty: Do you think it's all right for a girl to be making out with boys at the age of 16, whether or not she's "in love"?

Ruth: Well, I may not represent the normal sample, but I don't think it's a big deal if a girl becomes sexually active at the age of 16. After all, how old were you when you got started?

Betty: I'm afraid that I was a prude, and I guess I still am. But I never did it with anyone before I met Steve, the father of my children. I have to admit I was only 17, but until we got divorced, he was the only one.

Ruth: I hope it doesn't change your opinion of me if I tell you that I was a little more active than that. You might say that I was busy. I don't think that was necessarily good for me. In fact, I've always felt kind of bad about it. You know, all that baloney about "Nice girls don't . . ." Weren't you confused about where to draw the line when you were a teenager?

Betty: Sure. My parents told me not to go too far, but nobody ever said just how far that was. I must say, I was poorly informed as a teenager. I mean, I knew how you got pregnant, but I felt that could never happen to me because I just wouldn't have sex until I met someone I wanted to marry. But Steve was persistent, and after a while I got carried away too. Soon after that, Martha was conceived.

Ruth: You mean you had to get married?

Betty: Well, not when I was 17. But I got pregnant the summer after I graduated from high school. If I had known then that I would be supporting myself and my kids for most of my life, and if I hadn't been so much in love, then maybe I would have waited and everything would have turned out differently.

Ruth: But with birth control being so accessible today, nobody has to get pregnant unless they want to.

Betty: Maybe so, but I'm not about to tell Martha to go on the pill so she won't get pregnant. I mean, isn't that like encouraging her to have intercourse? I don't think she's sexually active yet. At least I certainly hope not. And if I tell her to get on the pill just in case she gets carried away, it seems like I would be telling her that I don't care what she does.

Ruth: I can see what you mean. But think of it this way. You have to weigh the risk of giving information against the risk of an unplanned pregnancy. On the other hand, I don't have a daughter. I look at it more from the perspective of a mother with a son. The one good thing you can say for boys is that they don't get pregnant! (They share another laugh.)

Betty: So for now, anyway, let's talk about birth control in terms of the big no. Next week we can talk about tubal ligations. (They laugh.) What do you think is the best way for a girl to say no? What did you do?

Ruth: Well, if I didn't want to get involved with a boy, I just made sure that we never even got started, if you know what I mean.

Betty: I agree with that, and I think it is important to have standards for what is permitted and what is not. For example, I think there's nothing wrong with kissing, but petting is different. Don't you think that petting leads to experimenting with sex?

Ruth: It might, but for heaven's sake, Betty, we're not living in the Victorian era. Kids today are in a hurry. If you are trying to teach your daughter to live with values that are out of date, she will stop listening to you.

Betty: I'm not sure I agree with you. But I also know that the thought of my daughter getting involved with a boy on any level is difficult for me. It's just hard to let go. And besides, I still think that it would be better for her self-esteem if she didn't just give it away to anyone who asks for it.

Ruth: I agree with you there. A girl should think enough of herself to decide, *in advance,* just how much of her sexuality she is willing to share with someone. And if she's going to give anything of herself to another person, he damned well better be worth it.

Betty: What do you tell your boys about sex? Do you believe in the double standard?

Ruth: I don't know if it's a double standard, but I do think that most boys start experimenting with sex in high school. I have talked to my son about promiscuity, the dangers of sexually transmitted diseases and AIDS, and the importance of birth control. We even talked specifically about how to use condoms. Did you know that condoms are much more effective when they are used with foam?

Betty: No. But I do know that condoms can reduce the risk of getting sexually transmitted diseases.

Ruth: Well, you should have heard our conversation. There was all this hooting and laughing when I suggested using foam, because that would mean planning ahead. And they said you never know when you're going to "get lucky."

Betty: (shaking her head in disgust) These kids! They think they are adults, but if you try to discuss something on an adult level, forget it.

Ruth: My basic message was that sex should be saved for intimate relationships. If you have a special relationship, you should be able to talk about contraceptives before you hop into bed together.

These conversations with Ruth became a regular occurrence. It really helped to have someone Betty could share her concerns with. She had two kids to raise by herself and she needed outside resources to help her deal with important issues such as sex, drugs, and fast cars—all the wild and crazy things that teenagers are exposed to these days.

Betty had lived a sheltered life until she was divorced. She went directly from living with her parents to living with her husband, Steve. She had never been on her own before Steve walked out on her. Then she had to get a job. She had a terrible time simply arranging baby-sitting for her children. Her mother had always been at home, and she had planned to do the same for her kids. She remembered feeling like a failure when she took the kids to the first (although not the last) daycare center. Martha and Ricky didn't make it easy on her—they cried when it was time for her to go. She couldn't forget the expression on their faces when she turned her back on them, got in the car, and drove away to her new job.

While Betty realized that she couldn't be the kind of mother she had once hoped to be, she still wanted to give her children a good start on life. It was often difficult for her to control Martha and Ricky. When she asked them to do something, it seemed as though they didn't hear her at all. Being a single parent didn't help much either because there was no one to support her attempts at discipline. Betty was a sensitive mother who loved her children, and she tried hard to teach them by encouraging them along the right path. She wanted them to learn how to be responsible adults without shoving morality at them. She wasn't always successful, but sometimes they paid attention. There were times when she heard her children advocating her ideas, even using the same words she had used, and this was reassuring.

Betty thought about the issue of sex and what she wanted to communicate to her kids. Over the years, she had talked to each of them about it on several occasions, sometimes alone and at other times together. She found that the best way to influence them was to discuss the important aspects of sexual behavior before the issue came up. Martha and Ricky seemed more open then. Her friends were concerned about the same issues, and they enjoyed sharing their thoughts on the subject. Betty was amazed at the range of perspectives among her friends. She noticed that parents with daughters were more conservative about sex than parents who didn't have daughters. Everyone seemed to agree that girls need more protection than boys, if only for the obvious reason that they can become pregnant. Quite a few parents said they thought boys should be taught to be as responsible about sex as girls.

With practice, it became easier for Betty to discuss these issues with her children. Her first attempts seemed stilted and difficult, and the kids acted like it was a big deal—they couldn't stop snickering and giggling. After a while, things changed and talking about sex was almost as easy as discussing any other topic. Betty was glad she had decided to bring the issue of sex into the open. Now she felt that she was in a much better position to help her adolescents make good choices about experimenting with sex.

Act IV: Betty Bares the Facts

The Scene. The family is riding in the car again. This time, however, Martha is driving. Martha, who is now 17 years old and a senior in high school, has her driver's license and loves to take the wheel when she is given the opportunity. The following scene takes place as Ricky, who is now 16, asks some rather personal questions about Betty's sex life with their father.

Ricky: So when did you start making it with Dad? Did you guys wait until after you were married?

Mom: (She gasps to herself. She has thought about how to answer this question and had decided to just lie about it. But now that the question has actually come up, she knows that it would be better to tell the truth. After all, if the children can't believe their own mother, who can they believe? After a long pause, she sighs and begins her story.) Well, no. We started "making it," as you say, when we were still in high school.

Martha: How old were you?

Mom: Don't I get to have any privacy about my teenage years at all? I'll make a deal with you—I'll tell you the truth, but I don't have to tell you everything, OK?

Both kids agree to this rule. They are glad to have their mother tell them anything at all.

Mom: Your dad was my first boyfriend, and he was the only boyfriend I ever had until after we were divorced. We went steady almost all the way through high school. We were tempted to "make it" for a long, long time before we finally gave in. I'm not trying to make excuses for myself, but it took *years,* not weeks or months, before we made our decision. (She pauses and thinks for a while, and then smiles to herself.) Maybe it was only a matter of months.

Martha: What did you use for birth control?

Mom: That was a bit of a problem. Back then there weren't as many different kinds of birth control as there are now. And everything was harder to get. We even had trouble getting information about birth control. My parents didn't tell me anything about contraceptives at all.

Martha: So what did you do?

Mom: We used condoms and coitus interruptus.

Ricky: What's that? It sounds like some sort of disease.

Martha: (to Ricky) That means the boy pulls his penis out before he ejaculates so the girl doesn't get pregnant. (then to her mother) What are the different kinds of birth control? Which ones are the most effective?

Betty is thankful she has thought about this ahead of time. She visited Planned Parenthood again a few months ago to find out about the contraceptives that are available for teenagers and received information about the pros and cons of each one. She also discussed this with their family doctor.

Mom: Well, I'm not an expert on this, but I do know a few of the basics. There are a number of ways to be safe. The best way, from my point of view, is not to have sex with anyone. For Martha, that means knowing how and when to say no, and for Ricky that means not being pushy with his girlfriends and maybe, nowadays, knowing when to say no. (Everyone laughs at this.) The method we just talked about, coitus interruptus, is not effective. It takes only a tiny drop of semen to fertilize an egg, and there is a small discharge of semen that can escape during heavy petting or just before the boy ejaculates.

Martha: What about the rhythm method? How does that work?

Mom: The rhythm method is based on the idea that women are only fertile for about three or four days each month, right in the middle of the menstrual cycle. If you track your periods carefully, it will tell you when the risky time is. But this method is not particularly effective either, especially if the woman has an irregular period. Still, it's better than nothing at all.

Ricky: What about rubbers? They work pretty well, don't they?

Mom: Well, yes and no. Condoms are effective if they are not defective and are used correctly. They are particularly effective if they are used with foam. But it takes some practice to learn how to use a condom properly. You should try putting them on several times alone so you will know how to use them in the heat of the moment. Condoms have the added advantage of providing some protection against AIDS and other sexually transmitted diseases.

Martha: What about using a diaphragm or the pill?

Mom: Diaphragms work, but it takes practice to use them properly. And for extra protection, it is usually necessary to use a spermicidal foam or gel with them. Then there is always the pill. But you have to remember to take the pills regularly, which is every day. If you forget to take them, you can get pregnant. Also, there may be some side effects from taking the pill.

Martha: What do you use, Mom?

Mom: I had a tubal ligation several years ago.

Ricky: What's that?

Mom: It's a type of microsurgery where they used a laser beam to close my fallopian tubes. I'll never be able to get pregnant again.

Martha: That means you're stuck with just us, doesn't it?

Mom: That's right. You two are the only children in my future.

Ricky: Don't guys have something like that done too? John's father can't have any more children either. What do they call it?

Mom: A vasectomy.

Ricky: Yeah, that's it. A vasectomy.

Mom: They say you can have that reversed, but a tubal ligation is almost always permanent. Neither of these birth control methods is available to teenagers. Even though you may think that you will never want children, you may find that you feel quite differently about this when you are a little older.

Many parents are concerned that if they talk with their children about sex, it may encourage them to become sexually active. But this is not supported by the research conducted to date. Rather, parents who *do not* talk to their youngsters have an increased risk of an unwanted pregnancy occurring in the family.

Providing information does not necessarily imply that it is all right for teenagers to have intercourse, and it does give them a certain amount of protection. In order to be sexually responsible, adolescents need to know about the various types of contraceptives, where to get them, and how to use them effectively. Teenagers also need information about AIDS and other sexually transmitted diseases so they can be aware of the risks connected with promiscuous behavior.

Teenagers say that the arguments most likely to influence their sexual activity included the dangers of catching a sexually transmitted disease and the impact of an unplanned pregnancy. They also say that free birth control and guaranteed confidentiality would increase the likelihood that they would be more consistent about using it.

Monitoring your adolescent is another important aspect of preventing inappropriate sexual activities (see Chapter 3 in *Part 1: The Basics* for additional information on monitoring). Adolescents who are carefully monitored by their parents can undoubtedly find an opportunity for a sexual encounter, but long periods of unsupervised time (for example, a weekend) make it possible for *many* such encounters to take place. In our own family, this is where the line was drawn. We did everything we could to set reasonable limits on the amount of unsupervised time that was available to our teenage children.

Act I: I Want to Spend the Night

The Scene. The room contains a strange mixture of objects that tell a great deal about the person who lives in it. The bed is a futon on the floor covered with an Indian-print bedspread. There are pillows of all sizes and shapes around the edge of the bed. On one of the pillows there is a tattered old teddy bear that is left over from another time but not yet abandoned. School books are piled on the floor by the door. A comfortable chair is draped with several scarves and some pantyhose, and the walls are covered with posters that do not have a consistent theme: Humphrey Bogart, a ballerina, a rock star, and a skier poised in mid-air. A cheap CD player stands in the corner with several boxes of CDs heaped around it. A few articles of clothing are strewn across the floor—it is hard to tell if they are dirty or clean. Martha is sprawled across the bed having an intense discussion with her best friend, Carole.

Martha: It looks like I can't go to Seattle next weekend. My mother is being totally weird. I don't know what she thinks she's preventing by not letting me go. It's like her whole number with curfews, too. She thinks that if I have to be home by 1 A.M. I won't be able to get it on with George. I told her that I could do it at nine o'clock in the morning if I wanted to. Just by setting these dumb curfews she thinks she is keeping me out of bed with George. That's stupid!

Carole: Why did you tell her you were going with George?

Martha: I didn't, but she guessed it. And she can always tell when I'm not telling the truth.

Carole: Well it's your own fault, then.

Martha: But she's being really stupid about it. This time next year I'll be out of this damned house, and what can she do then?

Carole: What did she say to that?

Martha: She said that next year I can do what I want. But while I'm living in her house, I have to follow her rules. I told her I'd be glad to move out now so she doesn't have to go through the hassle of holding the key to my chastity belt.

Carole: All right! What did she say to that?

Martha: Nothing. She kind of smirked and left for work. That's what drives me nuts about her. I can hardly ever get her to fight it out with me.

Carole: So what are you going to do? What does George say?

Martha: Well, actually, everything worked out because he couldn't go either. His car broke down again and he needs the money to buy parts, so we're planning to go next month. That'll give me more time to work on a better story to tell her. In the meantime, I'm stuck in this boring hole.

One thing that is fairly consistent about adolescents is that they can revise their plans *when it suits them.* They may fight you tooth and nail about an issue that they insist must be resolved in their favor, only to give up on it because one of their friends has had a change in plans. *Adolescents usually consider only the immediate present and fail to see the long-term consequences.* That is why it is so important for parents to do some of the long-range thinking for them and to set limits on their activities. Sometimes these limits are actually welcomed by the adolescent, who can use them to stay away from situations where there may be trouble. If the parent doesn't say no, how can the teenager?

Act II: Betty Sets the Rules

The Scene. Martha and her mother are having a heated discussion in the living room. It is Saturday morning, and last night Martha didn't come home until 3 A.M., which is two hours past her curfew. The following exchange takes place as Martha introduces her plan to go out tonight as well.

Mom: Well, as far as I'm concerned, you're not going out tonight until you do three hours of work for coming in late last night. Our agreement is that you will do one and a half minutes of work for every minute you are late.

Martha: But even if I do that, you're still going to insist on that stupid one o'clock curfew for tonight again, aren't you?

Mom: That's right. You only get to stay out later if there is something special happening—otherwise, I want you home by one o'clock. The movies are over at 11, and two hours is plenty of time to say goodnight to George.

Martha: After the movies we go out to get something to eat. All you can think about is me and George making out somewhere.

Mom: Martha, you know what my position is on that. I want you home by one o'clock because I don't want you out on the streets in the middle of the night. The kinds of things that go on at that time of the night have nothing to do with teenagers, so I'm not going to change the one o'clock rule. And, if you don't put in the three hours of work for last night, you won't be going out at all tonight.

Martha: As long as we are on the subject of sex, just what is it that you think you are protecting me from? I am not a virgin anymore, you know, so that's a lost cause.

Mom: It is my position that sex is for grown-ups. That means when you are responsible for yourself, you can make your own decisions about sex. I know that I can't keep you from sneaking around behind my back, but if I catch you, there will be a consequence. In the meantime, I don't plan to make it easy for you to sneak off with George or anyone else.

Martha: You must be living in some other century. I don't know of any other parents who are as old-fashioned as you are.

Mom: Well, I guess that's the breaks. I'm sorry, but you are stuck with me and my old-fashioned values until you leave home.

Commentary

You may have noticed that this was not a problem-solving session in which Betty was open to Martha's input. There are times when parents must set a rule and enforce it, even it if proves to be unpopular. Don't expect to be thanked by your kids for doing this, at least not for a few years. In this situation it is best to keep your discussions brief and to the point, especially if the issue or situation is a sensitive one. When two people take opposite positions on something and have strong feelings about it, there is no way to win with words.

Consequences for Sexually Related Behaviors

Parents rarely catch their adolescents engaging in sexual activities. For this reason, parents are forced to rely on circumstantial evidence indicating that the rules about sexual behavior have been broken. Your home is not a court of law, and circumstantial evidence is admissable and should be acted upon. What is some of the circumstantial evidence you should be looking for? Long periods of time when teenagers are not supervised by adults (other than legitimate extracurricular activities) are high-risk times. Too much free time makes it tempting for adolescents to experiment with sex and use drugs, or hang out with a delinquent peer group. If your son tells you he is going to the YMCA to work out with the swimming team, check out his story. Stop by sometime during practice. Talk to the coach about your youngster's progress. The purpose is not just to check on their whereabouts, but also to stay in touch with the world of your teenager. Who are the people you see hanging around the places your son frequents?

Adolescents should have to earn unsupervised time by demonstrating that they are responsible and can be trusted. As your children grow older, they will gradually learn to make good choices about how to spend their free time. If they make poor decisions, don't allow much unsupervised time. When they show that they can make good choices, give them more freedom as a reward. Leaving teenagers alone overnight is asking for some very responsible behavior on their part. It takes practice to learn to resist temptation. If they sometimes fail to live up to your expectations, don't give up, and don't overreact. Simply impose a reasonable consequence, and put some restrictions on their freedom for a short period of time.

Then make it clear that they will have to earn their freedom back by showing you that they can behave in a responsible manner when you are not there.

Another type of circumstantial evidence is noticing that someone has been using your bed. The next teaching drama illustrates one way to handle this situation.

Act I: Who's Been Sleeping in My Bed?

Marissa, the mother, has to work all day. She has two children, a 16-year-old son, George, and a 12-year-old son, Mark. She monitors her children during the day by telephone and by going home for quick lunches. Summer vacations are particularly hard on Mom because her two boys are too old for a baby-sitter.

The Scene. When Mom came home from work this evening, she noticed that her bed had been used. The evidence suggested something more than someone sitting on top of the bed. She could tell that someone had been between the sheets, and she was furious. Mom knew what probably had happened, and she was shocked that her son could be so tacky. The following conversation takes place as Mom confronts George with the evidence.

Mom: How could you use my bed? You make me sick to my stomach! (She stands in the kitchen, her hands clenched at her sides, tears streaming down her face. She is so upset that she is shaking all over. Neither of her kids can remember ever seeing her so upset. Even Marissa is surprised at how angry she feels. Does she really expect her son to remain innocent forever? No, it isn't that. It is more that she feels betrayed. Her bedroom is her one place of solitude, her inner sanctum. Using her bed was disrespectful, and it makes her feel like she can't trust George anymore. And the fact that he didn't even try to hide the evidence is a slap in the face. There are plenty of other beds in the house. Why did he have to use hers?)

George: Take it easy, Mom. You're overreacting. I'm sorry—
it'll never happen again.

Mom: I don't even want to see your face. Just go to your room
and stay there. You make me sick.

George and Mom went to their own rooms and shut the doors.
The younger boy, Mark, went to a friend's house in the neighbor-
hood. Mom started to lie down on her bed but stopped when she
remembered what happened there. After a few minutes she marched
into George's room and ordered him to change her sheets. Then she
left the apartment for a long walk. The walk helped her to calm
down. Afterwards, she realized that her anger had gotten out of control. This wasn't the end of the world, even though it felt like it at
the time. It was easier for her to think now that she was feeling less
upset, but she still didn't know what to do about the situation. It was
clear that she had to do something, but she didn't think she could
be rational about it until later, so she decided to tell George that he
was grounded until an appropriate consequence was set. Why
should she be in a hurry? In the meantime, she could mull it over
for a while. She talked about it with her sister, who had two
teenagers of her own. She even talked about it with her mother.
Everyone she talked to seemed to have strong opinions about what
she should do. Some advised her to ground him until the summer
was over, but the thought of having to put up with George moping
around the house for an entire summer seemed intolerable to her.
That idea was quickly rejected.

Finally, Mom decided to write a list of possible consequences:
1. Do nothing.
2. Ground him:
   a. forever.
   b. for a month.
   c. for a week.
3. Yell at him.
4. Call up the girl's mother and talk to her.
5. Give him a work consequence.
6. Take away his car privileges.

7. Don't let him play football in the fall.
8. Restrict him from seeing the girl who was with him.
9. Charge him a fine.
10. Make him do some charitable deed, like volunteering at a senior center or baby-sitting for his aunt.
11. Have him write an essay on morality.
12. Take away his telephone privileges.
13. Get a "baby-sitter" to monitor his activities while she is at work.

She found that it helped a lot to think about the possible consequences because it made her feel as though she was regaining some control over the situation. It took her two days to make up her mind about what to do. Finally, she decided to have him clean the entire apartment, from top to bottom. She wanted the windows washed, the shower tiles scrubbed free of scum. She wanted the oven cleaned and all the floors mopped and vacuumed. She spent one enjoyable evening alone in her room making out the list of work she wanted him to complete.

The next thing she did was to call the mother of the girl who was involved. She knew that if some other parents had caught their daughter with her son, she would want to know about it. So she called the mother and explained what had happened. George had an absolute fit about that, but she told him that he should have thought about that before he took the liberty of using her bed.

George was grounded until he finished all of the chores. It took him three days to finish the work. While he was doing it, Mom made sure that she stayed out of his way. Every now and then she would see him scurrying around the house with his dust rags and squeegee. George actually looked relieved when she told him about the consequence she had assigned, and he willingly did the work.

Ultimately, it is up to each parent to decide what an appropriate consequence might be for a particular problem behavior. In general, a consequence should not last longer than a week or two at the most. When punishments last longer than that, they are difficult to monitor, and it allows too much adolescent anger to build up. Good consequences are immediate and not too intense, and they should be applied consistently and contingently. (More information on setting consequences is provided in Chapter 6 of *Part 1: The Basics.*)

Key Ideas in This Chapter

1. Evaluate your current status in teaching sexual responsibility to your youngsters. Prepare in advance how you will talk to your children about sex in a way that fits their current level of understanding.
2. Communicate accurate information in a straightforward and unemotional manner.
3. Talk to your children about issues of sexuality *before* you are confronted with a problem. They will be much more open to listening to you before they have become involved. Even though your discussion may be stilted and uncomfortable at first, your ability to talk openly about sexual responsibility will improve with practice.
4. Provide age-appropriate reading material.
5. Monitor your children. Do not allow long periods of time without adult supervision.
6. Discuss your concerns with other adults, including friends, other parents, ministers, etc.
7. Recognize that parents with daughters may have different perspectives than those with sons.
8. Don't expect your youngsters to thank you for slowing down their sexual activities.
9. Provide reasonable consequences for infractions of your rules. Do not use guilt. (See Chapter 6 in *Part 1: The Basics.*)
10. Offer a certain amount of information about your own sexual development. Be discreet, but share some of the feelings and concerns you had when you were an adolescent.

Chapter Six Homework Assignment

1. Gather information so you can pass it on to your teenagers. Contact the public library and talk to the children's librarian. He or she can suggest some books that will help. Look through

several books, and select the ones that fit your values and that are age appropriate. You may also want to contact Planned Parenthood. They can give you information about birth control methods and sound advice on preventing sexually transmitted diseases and AIDS. They may also have brochures that you can leave around the house.

2. Plan in advance how you will discuss sexuality. Try some of the methods mentioned earlier in this chapter (rehearse in front of a mirror, audiotape or practice your presentation with your spouse, a friend, etc.).

3. If you think it is time, present some basic information to your children. Remember: It is better to be too early than too late.

4. Discuss with other adults the idea of giving teenagers information about sexuality and birth control.

CHAPTER 7

ˈgs and Alcohol

ˈng up in a society where there is widespread use of drugs and alcohol. Through their parents, the media, and their peers, adolescents are routinely exposed to a variety of licit and illicit drugs. From caffeine, nicotine, and prescription medications to marijuana, methamphetamine, and crack cocaine—drugs have crept into all levels of our society. In addition, the media convey mixed messages about drugs and alcohol. On one hand, public-service announcements tell children to "Just Say No." On the other hand, television commercials, billboards, and advertisements in newspapers and magazines make alcohol and tobacco seem very appealing. Attractive young adults are shown intimately sipping wine coolers or tipping back glasses overflowing with ice cold beer in crowded bars. Children see their parents and other adults habitually using their drugs of choice: drinking several cups of strong coffee to wake up in the morning, smoking cigarettes throughout the day, having a drink or two to relax after work, or taking a pill to help them sleep at night. One part of our society condemns such use, while another segment condones it. In the midst

165

of this ambivalence, it is difficult for parents to teach their children to make responsible choices about drugs and alcohol.

In spite of the fact that it is illegal for minors to have alcohol or drugs in their possession, the majority of teenagers do try alcohol and cigarettes, and many of them get involved with illicit drugs such as marijuana, Ecstasy, and cocaine. Efforts directed at controlling access to alcohol and addictive or mind-altering substances are worthwhile, but it is also important for parents to take an active role in monitoring their adolescent's activities and choice of friends.

For most parents, the real concern is that *experimenting* with drugs and alcohol will lead to substance abuse. While a professional should probably be involved if your adolescent is a substance abuser, it is the parents who are primarily responsible for preventing their adolescents from going beyond the threshold of experimentation. The problem of substance abuse develops slowly, and there are many small steps in the progression. It is important for parents to be aware of these steps so they can intervene before the situation becomes serious. This chapter presents a brief summary of findings from some recently completed studies of adolescent drug and alcohol use, and outlines an approach that can help parents to prevent their teenagers from falling into patterns of abuse.

Four Danger Signs

Four factors place an adolescent at risk for substance abuse: early, regular use of drugs and/or alcohol; truancy and school failure; hanging out with deviant peers; and lack of parental monitoring. Adolescents with all four risk factors have the highest likelihood of becoming substance abusers. These danger signs mean your adolescent is gambling with the odds, and losing the gamble could have dire consequences.

Although studies strongly suggest that the regular use of drugs or alcohol *at an early age* can lead to substance abuse. But it is important to note that *most* adolescents who are early users do not go on to become substance abusers. For many adolescents, the early start is related to thrill seeking and is part of being deeply involved with a peer group. If adolescents are socially skilled, the drugs and alcohol are not the primary focus of the positive experiences they have with their friends. For the most part, adolescents go to parties to socialize, and the drugs and alcohol are incidental to the situation.

Failing at school is also a risk factor for adolescent substance abuse. The connection here is perhaps less obvious, but there are several possible explanations. Skipping classes, lack of motivation, and having a "bad attitude" can all contribute to poor academic performance. Skipping classes provides unsupervised time to hang out with peers who are doing likewise, and this is an invitation to get into trouble. Adolescents who don't do well in school may also have difficulty working toward long-range goals and delaying gratification, which are necessary skills for academic achievement. Since substance use provides immediate gratification, it may be particularly attractive to those who fail at school. The cavalier "I don't care" attitude evident in many adolescents who fail at school would also tie into substance abuse. These teenagers are less reluctant to try new and daring experiences because they feel they have little to lose.

A third factor relating to substance use is spending time with a deviant peer group. Deviant peers are antisocial children who push the limits in every setting. When they are in school they test the rules, fail to complete work, and receive poor grades. Antisocial teenagers tend to have truancy problems and spend a great deal of time in unsupervised activities. In many cases, these adolescents have been picked up by the police, some on more than one occasion. They are intent upon showing the world that the rules that apply to others don't apply to them. Instead of the relatively normal pattern of experimenting with substance use, they quickly escalate to substance abuse. Hanging out with a deviant peer group increases the likelihood that your adolescent will have a problem with alcohol and drug abuse.

Parents who do not provide adequate supervision may one day find that their adolescent has a problem with substance abuse. If parents fail to monitor their adolescent's peers, activities, and school performance, it means there are ample opportunities for their adolescent to drift into patterns of alcohol and drug abuse.

The presence of all four risk factors doesn't *guarantee* that a particular adolescent will become a substance abuser, but these are warning signals that parents should take seriously. There is no reason to watch from the sidelines as adolescents develop habits that can interfere with their lives as adults. The next section outlines some strategies you can use to prevent your adolescent from becoming a substance abuser.

Preventing Substance Abuse

The studies conducted at the Oregon Social Learning Center suggest there are three things parents can do to reduce the risk of their adolescents becoming substance abusers: monitor them carefully, limit their freedom to spend time with deviant peers, and help them do well in school.

Monitoring

Our research suggests that it is important for parents to carefully monitor their adolescents' activities. Monitoring involves knowing the answers to four basic questions: Who are your children with? What are they doing? Where are they? When will they be home? (The process of monitoring is described in detail in Chapter 3 of *Part 1: The Basics.*)

Your house rules should require adolescents to tell you where they are going, who they will be with, how they are getting there and back, and what time they will be home. Then pay attention to whether the information they provide is accurate. This means doing some occasional checking. You can keep your investigations low-profile, and if your adolescents are doing as they said, they won't really mind. When your checkups consistently point to responsible behavior, you can become less vigilant, but never give up the occasional spot check. If you find they have been lying to you, set a consequence for it and track them more carefully for a while.

When the authors' children were adolescents, we monitored their activities without being overly restrictive and paid attention to who their friends were. We also tried to make sure their activities with peers were supervised by an adult. In all honesty, we were not always completely successful. It is difficult to consistently track what adolescents are doing, and it seems as though they spend a great deal of energy thinking of ways to push the rules without getting caught. There were times when one of our teenagers would do something that would catch us completely off guard because we were immersed in crises of our own. When we realized what was going on, some extra effort was required to bring the situation back within the normal range. These "catching up" periods inevitably led to confrontations, which in turn led to changes in the house rules and the consequences for breaking them. It also meant that we had to pay more attention to the positive aspects of family life. It is important for parents to try to stay on top of things and to be flexible enough to make the changes necessary to deal with any situation that may arise.

Deviant Peers

The second area of intervention for parents who are concerned about their adolescent's substance use involves peers. What can you do if your adolescent is spending time with a deviant peer group? There isn't an easy answer to this question, but the following are several ideas you might consider.

1. Get together with some other adults and find out how they manage problems with deviant peers.
2. Limit the time adolescents are allowed to spend with rowdy or antisocial peers.
3. Provide extra supervision.
4. Get adolescents involved in extracurricular activities where they learn new skills and make new friends. There will be very few antisocial teenagers there, because they tend to avoid learning new skills or cooperating with others in groups.
5. Spend time doing things with your adolescent that you both enjoy (build up the "interpersonal bank account").

6. Encourage adolescents to bring their friends home.
7. Maintain some contact with the parents of their friends.
8. Occasionally provide transportation to and from activities, and try to get other parents to take turns with you.
9. When you go on family outings, let your adolescent bring a friend along sometimes.

Academic Performance

The third area of concern is academic achievement. It is up to parents to make sure their children do reasonably well in school. If their report cards indicate they are having problems, do something about it. Some guidelines for contracting with adolescents to keep up with their schoolwork are described in the next chapter.

Some Practical Steps for Parents

The procedures for controlling adolescent drug and alcohol use are similar to those that have been presented for dealing with other problems. Step one is to think carefully about your position on drug and alcohol use, and to establish house rules that clearly specify what is allowed and what is not. Then define your goals based on what your child is doing now, and outline your plan to achieve them. Step two is to set up positive consequences for compliance and negative consequences for rule violations. Step three is to write down the rules and the consequences, and discuss them with your adolescent. Step four is to carefully monitor your adolescent's behavior and activities. Step five is to evaluate the effectiveness of your course of action and do some fine-tuning if necessary.

The first step is to discuss your position on the use of intoxicating substances with your spouse or partner. If each of you has a different perspective, use the rules for communication to send and receive information, do some brainstorming, and then evaluate the list of possibilities. It is important to present a unified front on the issue of drugs and alcohol. Try to reach an agreement about the approach you will use, and establish some rules.

Make sure your rules are realistic and enforceable. There is little sense in creating rules that you cannot enforce. It may be tempting to make a statement like "No child of mine will *ever* use drugs or alcohol, or be in the same room with someone who does." Even if this is what you *want,* it is not a realistic approach to the problem. It is better to establish a rule that is enforceable. For example, "Drinking or using illegal drugs is not permitted in our home. Possession of alcohol or drugs is not allowed, and any signs of using them will result in a consequence." Then specify the consequence. A rule like this makes your position clear and makes it possible to punish violations. It is a warning to adolescents that they'd better have enough self-control not to stagger home drunk or stoned. The message is, "If you are experimenting with alcohol or drugs, keep it under control so there isn't any evidence of it, or else there will be consequences." This is not the same as saying that it's all right to use alcohol and drugs.

It is important for parents to make it clear to their teenagers *what* age is too early to start, *where* the use of drugs and alcohol is not permitted, and *what* kinds of substances are dangerous to experiment with. It is your responsibility to take a position on these issues and to make that position known to your adolescent. Most teenagers are in contact with drugs and alcohol, and they need to know how to handle tempting situations when you aren't there to help them make the right choices.

Step two is to set up some positive and negative consequences to back up your rules. Talking to adolescents has little effect on their behavior—it takes consequences to change behavior. Specify the punishment for violating the rules about drugs and alcohol. Infractions should be handled by applying the prearranged consequences. This should be done in a matter-of-fact style without lecturing. The consequences should be something like a work detail, a fine subtracted from weekly allowances or wages earned, or loss of car privileges for a specific amount of time. You should also think about some rewards the adolescent can earn if there is no evidence of drug or alcohol use. Some examples might include helping with car insurance payments, use of the car on certain nights, or a monetary bonus each month. After doing some preliminary thinking about these issues, involve your adolescent in negotiating the details.

Step three is to write down the rules and consequences and discuss them with your adolescent. If you have other children and they are too young to understand the issue of drugs and alcohol, you may want to exclude them from the meeting. Describe your position, and present the new rules to your adolescent. Observe the rules for conducting family forums to prevent negative emotions from interfering with the process. The consequences for complying with the rules and for breaking them should be clearly specified. Keep the guidelines for introducing sensitive issues in mind when you are doing this. When you have agreed on the rules and consequences, write them down for future reference.

Step four is to look for signs that your adolescent is using alcohol or drugs. Some of these signs can be detected by tracking your adolescent's mood and behavior. On a general level, pay attention to whether he or she is happy or sad, responsive or despondent, involved or distant. Show some interest in his or her activities. The "How was your day?" exchanges that many parents have with their teenagers can provide some useful information about their general welfare. Even if everything seems all right, take a close look at how your adolescent is doing every once in a while. If it appears that trouble is brewing, begin tracking what is going on more carefully.

On a specific level, there are several things to look for. As we have already mentioned, one of the main areas of concern is the adolescent's peer group. Is your son or daughter frequently in contact with teenagers who are known to use drugs or alcohol regularly? There are also some physical signs that indicate drug and alcohol use. Have you noticed any changes in your adolescent's alertness, sleeping patterns, or activity levels? You should start to suspect that something is wrong if your adolescent is lethargic, shaky, jittery, startles easily, or has red eyes. Heavy drinking is usually followed by a hangover, so look for signs of this as well. If you notice the smell of alcohol or marijuana, there is little doubt about what is going on. If you don't know what marijuana smells like, ask a friend or acquaintance who uses it to let you smell the smoke. Paraphernalia such as roach clips, rolling papers, and small pipes (sometimes made out of the paper tube from a roll of toilet paper) are a sure sign that marijuana or hashish is being used. You should also be on the lookout for strange-looking pills, unfamiliar "vitamins," powdery substances wrapped in small papers, tiny bottles, syringes, and burned spoons.

One way to find out what is going on when adolescents are away from home is to pay attention to how they look when they come home. You should be particularly observant during the evening hours, since this is the time for parties. Make an effort to greet your adolescent in person instead of yelling hello from the back room. Without being nosy, try to talk to them when they come home. If you notice slurred speech, red eyes, or other signs of alcohol and drug use, then it is time for you to monitor their outside activities more closely. A word of caution—adolescents are naturally a little moody and "spacey," so don't interpret all such behaviors as signs of substance abuse; but consistent patterns deserve attention.

If you are looking for evidence of problems and find there is none, accept this as a positive sign. At the very least, this means your adolescent has enough self-control and respect for your rules to keep the evidence out of sight. It is difficult for adolescents who are regular substance users to do this. Even if you don't find any evidence, continue to monitor what is going on so that if a problem begins to develop it won't have a chance to get out of hand.

Step five is to evaluate your rules and backup consequences, and make any necessary changes. Let's say, for example, you have reason to suspect that your teenager is using illegal substances. Without stating your intentions, increase the rewards for following the rules and announce that signs of getting high will result in a specific punishment. Then carefully monitor your adolescent and provide consequences accordingly. Make it worthwhile for your adolescent to abide by the rules. In general, it is a good idea to select consequences that reflect the importance you attach to the behavior you are trying to change.

Taking a Position

There is tremendous variation in where parents draw the line on these important issues. Here are some examples: (1) absolutely no alcohol, marijuana, or other illegal substances allowed anywhere, at any time; (2) no use or evidence of alcohol, marijuana, or other drugs in the home; (3) the use of alcohol and marijuana is prohibited at inappropriate times and places (inappropriate times and places should then be defined; for example, before or during school, in public places, or while driving); (4) alcohol and/or marijuana may only be used at home (describe the circumstances); (5) alcohol and/or marijuana may only be used when an adult is present; (6) alcohol and/or marijuana may be used at the adolescent's discretion, but certain guidelines must be followed (for example, use substances in moderation, and don't drive when using even small amounts). Perhaps none of these rules fits your own system of values. The options listed above have been included to represent the broad range of possibilities.

It is important for you to make active decisions about these issues instead of waiting for a problem to arise before you make your position known. Consider how you feel about the issue, and discuss it with your spouse; or if you don't have a spouse, consult a friend, an adult family member, a minister, or some other confidant. Ask for some feedback on your approach. Are your rules reasonable ones that can be monitored? What should the consequences be for infractions? Do this *before* you talk to your adolescent. After you have made some decisions about your position, then sit down and discuss the issue with your adolescent.

Let's consider an example of a family dealing with the issue of substance use. We do not mean to imply that this is the way you should handle the problem; but it should be informative to watch another family in action.

Teddy Returns from a Night on the Town

The following drama involves the Blenders, a family we have met in a previous chapter. This time Riva and Ray have caught 17-

year-old Teddy (Riva's son by another marriage) coming home drunk one Saturday night. They have suspected for some time that Teddy has been drinking, smoking marijuana, and maybe using mind-altering drugs like LSD. Although there have been some signs of trouble, Riva and Ray have been afraid to do anything about it because they aren't sure how to approach the problem. They have been worried that a confrontation will signal the beginning of a long-standing conflict or that they might find out Teddy is involved with "hard" drugs. On this particular Saturday night, it is clear that Teddy has been driving while intoxicated.

When Teddy came home drunk, there was a terrible scene. Riva was crying, and Ray was making threats. Teddy was so out of it that he didn't respond much, except to laugh inappropriately. Finally, Teddy fell asleep fully dressed at one or two o'clock in the morning. It was clear that Teddy had been driving while intoxicated, and this situation worried Riva and Ray enough to force them to take action.

Act I: The Summit Meeting

The Scene. It's the day after Teddy's incident, and Riva and Ray are sitting in a restaurant having dinner together. The topic of discussion is what to do about Teddy.

Riva: What are we going to do about this? You know how I feel about teenagers drinking—as far as I'm concerned it's completely out of the question. Obviously, Teddy doesn't know how to control it. And the fact that he was stupid enough to drive when he was that intoxicated is outrageous.

Ray: I agree with you for the most part. Teddy certainly showed a lack of judgment by driving in that condition, and we need to set a strong consequence for that. But I also think that it is normal for a boy his age to do *some* drinking. He is 17 years old, after all. Next year he's going to be on his own, and then we won't have any influence on him. Do you really think we can keep him from ever drinking again?

Riva: No, probably not.

Ray: And how successful do you think we could be at making him stop?

Riva: Not very.

Ray: So do you still think we should try to get him to stop completely?

Riva: Yes! I really do!

Ray: Even though we both agree that it's not realistic?

Riva picks up the menu and reads it through a veil of tears. She is sniffling slightly as the waiter comes over and asks if they would like something to drink before dinner. They order a bottle of wine and continue their discussion.

Riva: I don't know how to deal with this. There doesn't seem to be a good answer. On one hand, I really feel he shouldn't drink at all; he's already shown us that he can't handle it. There is a law against drinking before the age of 21. And the fact that he was driving while he was drunk scares me—he could have hurt himself, or wrecked the car, or seriously hurt someone else. I guess if he had been picked up by the police they would have taken care of the driving problem for us—his license would have been automatically suspended, and he might have spent the night in jail. Maybe that would have taught him something.

Ray: Well, it sounds like you are suggesting that we should tell Teddy he can't have another drink until he's 21.

Riva: Yes, that's the way I feel about it right now. But I do agree with you that it's probably unrealistic and that we won't be able to enforce it.

Ray: Would you be willing to settle for something else?

The waiter arrives and begins to pour the wine. Riva and Ray watch silently; then they order dinner, and the discussion continues.

Riva: What would you suggest? I guess I just don't know what is reasonable any more. Look at us, for example. We're sitting here sipping wine while we discuss what to do about my son the drunkard.

Ray: Riva, he's not a drunkard because he came home drunk. What he has done is serious. But frankly, the thing I'm most concerned about is his drinking and driving. That is dangerous to himself and to others. I'm just glad that we caught him. What if we had been asleep when he came home? He might have gotten away with this. (Riva's eyes fill with tears again as she thinks about the possibilities. Ray continues in a gentle tone of voice.) If you get out the notepad, we can start listing the options that seem workable. Maybe that would help you feel less overwhelmed by this situation.

Riva and Ray worked on the list of options during the salad course and halfway through dinner. Their list consisted of the following:
1. No drinking ever again until he's 21.
2. No drinking as long as Teddy is living at home.
3. Drinking is only allowed when a responsible adult is present.
4. No drinking with his friends.
5. No signs of drinking are allowed (that is, beer cans or hard liquor bottles either empty or full, hanging out with kids who drink, or coming home smelling of alcohol, and so on).
6. Begin teaching Teddy responsible drinking patterns at home.

Ray: Which of these options do you like best?

Riva: You know I like the no drinking until 21 option, but I have to agree with you that we won't be able to enforce that one. The idea about not drinking until he leaves home makes me nervous because it makes it easy to avoid the problem for now, but he may still develop a drinking problem later on. Neither of these options teaches Teddy how to control his drinking. We should try to have an impact on the problem while he is at home and we still have some influence over him. I am starting to come around to the idea of teaching him responsible drinking habits. The only problem I see with that is it seems like we're encouraging him to drink. He is a minor, and that could mean we would be breaking the law.

Ray: I don't think so. Not in this state.

Riva: I hope you're right. Otherwise, I can see the headlines now: "Parents Force Alcohol on Teenage Son While Attempting to Teach Drinking Skills."

They have a good laugh together. The waiter comes by, clears their plates away, and pours them another glass of wine.

Ray: Do you see any point in going over the pros and cons of all these options, or do you think we should start spelling out how to teach him responsible drinking?

Riva raises her glass and proposes a toast to responsible drinking.

Commentary

Again, we want to emphasize that it is up to each set of parents to establish their own position on the issue of using intoxicating substances. Riva and Ray are correct in suggesting that teaching their adolescent about responsible drinking in their own home is a crime in many states. Their position is not necessarily the best one, but it is the option that seemed the most realistic to them. Let's see how they spell it out.

Ray: What is responsible drinking, and how do we teach it to a 17-year-old high school senior?

Riva: I guess it means teaching Teddy how to drink without getting drunk.

Ray: Well, for one thing, we don't gulp down large quantities of hard liquor or get involved in drinking contests and games.

Riva: Then let's make a rule about no hard liquor. Beer and wine are the only beverages allowed, and they should be consumed slowly, in sips instead of gulps. We need to teach Teddy to get some pleasure from tasting what he is drinking rather than drinking just to get high.

Ray: And the high—that's an important part of it. There is a big difference between drinking to the point where you feel good and then slowing down so you can maintain that feeling, instead of chugging it down until you get plastered.

Right now, for instance, we each have had three glasses of wine, which would get you drunk if you consumed it all at once, especially on an empty stomach. But it took us two hours to drink it with our dinner, so we didn't get drunk. I feel good, and my thinking seems clear.

Riva: But it might be hard to teach him how to know when he is getting a mild glow from alcohol. Teenagers seem to need to be hit over the head with something before they notice it. I mean, I agree with you, but maybe we should also teach him to keep track of the amount of alcohol he consumes per hour. I've heard MADD ads on the radio that say how drunk you get depends on how much you weigh and how much alcohol you consume over a certain period of time.

Ray: I use the rule of thumb that your body can metabolize alcohol at the rate of about one beer per hour. We could tell him about that. And what about teaching him to eat beforehand and while he's drinking? That can make a big difference in how high you get. One other important piece of information is that you don't feel the full effects of alcohol for about 45 minutes. So if you have been drinking heavily, it's a good idea to slow down for a while before drinking more. Otherwise, you can easily end up hugging the toilet bowl.

Riva: You know, in France, Spain, Italy, and other countries, kids have a little watered wine with their meals. They have some problems with alcoholism, but it does teach children that there are appropriate times for drinking when adults are around to monitor them. Maybe we should have a special dinner once a week, with candles, music, good conversation, and wine. To me, that's drinking with class!

Ray: (He smiles and rolls his eyes.) It sounds like you've been reading too many romance novels.

Riva: (Her expression shows that she didn't appreciate Ray's comment.) Well, Ray, if you have some suggestions, let's hear them. This is one way I think we can teach him about drinking when we're around.

Ray: OK—I take it back. Let's write down your suggestion. What do we have so far?

Teaching Teddy Responsible Drinking Patterns

1. Learn to drink without getting drunk.
2. No hard stuff; beer or wine only.
3. Take sips instead of gulps.
4. Teach him to taste what he is drinking.
5. Notice the glow from moderate drinking.
6. Present information about the amount of alcohol per hour.
7. Eat before and during drinking.
8. Have a fancy meal with wine once a month.

Ray: How about making him drink to get drunk several times in a row so he'll get sick and hate it? That's what they do to teach people to stop smoking.

Riva: That's a terrible idea. He'll just learn that it's all right to get drunk, and develop bad habits, and it's bad for his body, and . . .

Ray: (interrupting) All right, all right. Calm down. I just said that to see if you would react, and you did. But let's write it down anyway, because that's the rule.

Riva: (She reluctantly writes, 9. Drink until sick.) I've got an idea! Let's include something about driving. After all, that's one of the most important parts. We need to tell him what to do if he does get drunk when he's out with his friends.

Ray: I hate to think of the example we have set in the past. We're better about not driving when we drink now, but we haven't always been perfect.

Riva: Well, it's not our behavior that's in question right now. We'll try to set a better example for him by taking a taxi when we're out drinking with our friends.

Riva turns to a new page in the notebook and writes at the top: Drinking and Driving Rules. After much discussion and another glass of wine they came up with the following list:

1. No driving after drinking *anything* (or taking drugs of any sort), not even one beer or a single glass of wine.
2. No riding with anyone who has had *anything* to drink or any drugs.
3. If necessary, call a cab, and we will pay for it when you get home.
4. If necessary, call us in the middle of the night, and we will pick you up without a lecture. (Although there may be a consequence for drinking to get drunk.)

Ray: It's getting late, Riva. And if I have any more wine, we're going to have to call a cab. I think we're off to a good start here.

Riva: OK, honey, Let's go. We can keep thinking about this and add to the list later. It doesn't have to be perfect the first time.

Act II: Shootout in the Kitchen

The Scene. The next evening after dinner, Riva and Ray sit down with Teddy in the family room. The TV is off for the evening, and the other children have been asked not to interrupt them.

Ray: We need to talk to you about coming home drunk on Saturday, but I want to make it clear from the beginning that there are some ground rules that are to be observed here tonight, Teddy. This is going to be a civilized family meeting and the usual rules apply. That means we will not interrupt each other, and we will speak to each other in a respectful tone of voice. If anyone makes three nasty remarks, we will end the meeting. But you also need to know that you are completely grounded until we have this worked out, so it's in your best interest to hang in there. By the way, completely grounded means no car, no phone calls, and coming home from school within one hour. Do you understand?

Teddy is sitting on the edge of his chair, staring at the table. He barely nods his head to indicate that he understands. Ray considers demanding an answer but decides this is not important.

Riva: Ray and I have discussed your behavior the other night, and we are very concerned about your lack of good judgment. Getting drunk and then driving home is dangerous and inappropriate. We have decided to set some rules about drinking so that if this ever happens again, you will know the consequences in advance.

Ray: Because we are most concerned about drinking and driving, the consequences for that are the strongest. For Saturday night's incident, you have lost driving privileges for one month.

This gets Teddy's attention. His head snaps up and he glares at Ray. When Teddy begins to talk, his mother quickly holds up her hand to stop him.

Riva: Wait a minute, Teddy. I just want you to understand that this was *my* idea, not Ray's. In fact, I wanted to keep you from driving for the rest of the school year.

Teddy: You can't keep me from driving. I wasn't caught by the police. I still have my license and it's *my car,* so forget it. You two have nothing to do with my driving.

Riva: That's one mark for the nasty comment. The next thing for you to know is that there will be no drinking outside of this house. And you are not allowed to go to keggers or other parties where there is drinking. We do not accept the idea that it's all right to use drugs and alcohol at your age.

Teddy: Who's talking about drugs all of a sudden? I thought we were talking about drinking!

Riva: (The tension is evident in her tone of voice.) Technically, alcohol *is* a drug; and we don't want you to be drinking, smoking marijuana, or doing any of those other damned drugs, either. We won't have it, do you understand?

Ray: (gently) Riva, that's one mark for you. Let's try to stay calm about this. (Teddy smirks and Riva shoots a resentful glare at Ray, but Ray continues.) If we find out that you have been drinking or using drugs, the consequence will be three hours of work in the yard.

Teddy: (His face contorted in anger, he snarls through clenched teeth.) You can't *make* me do it, just like there's no way you can keep me from driving *my* car.

Riva: Watch your tone of voice, young man! That's strike two for you. The work chore you have earned for your performance last Saturday night is that you will completely clean up the backyard. I have made a list of everything I expect you to do. And until you have that job finished, there will be no privileges at all. When the job is done, all your privileges will be restored, with the exception of driving. You may not drive again until four weeks from last Saturday, which is May 4th.

Teddy jumps up from his seat and leaves the room, slamming the door behind him.

Ray: Well, I guess that's strike three, so the conversation is over. (with a friendly smile) We never did get to talk about your fancy dinners and wine tastings. Maybe next time . . . (He reaches over to give her a long hug, and they both breathe a deep sigh of relief to have this conversation over.)

Commentary

These parents have done an exceptional job of dealing with a difficult problem. They worked together to arrive at an approach that was agreeable to both of them. That is one of the keys to a successful outcome. If Riva and Ray were divided on the issue when they confronted Teddy, he probably would have gotten away with no consequences for his actions. Sometimes it seems as though adolescents have a sixth sense about where parents disagree, and they instinctively play on these differences. If the parents start to argue with each other, the adolescent has won. Notice that even though Riva and Ray initially had some differences on the issue of substance use, this was not apparent to Teddy. When the family meeting was called, Riva and Ray presented a united front.

Even though Riva and Ray did not actually "solve" the problem, they have made good progress. Their position has been clearly expressed to Teddy, and he probably realizes that he had better learn to be discreet. It may take several more discussions with Teddy before he does his chore and has his privileges reinstated.

Key Ideas in This Chapter

1. Adolescents are routinely exposed to alcohol and a wide variety of licit and illicit drugs.
2. Many adolescents *experiment* with alcohol and cigarettes, and some have used illicit drugs such as marijuana, but only a very small percentage go on to become substance *abusers*.
3. Parents need to make active decisions regarding how they feel about the use of alcohol, cigarettes, and illicit drugs by adolescents. Parents should then make their position clear to their adolescent before these issues come up.
4. There are four risk factors for substance abuse: early, regular use of alcohol and/or drugs; truancy and school failure; associating with deviant peers; and lack of parental monitoring.
5. Efforts by parents to intervene in patterns of abuse should focus on these risk factors.

Chapter Seven Homework Assignment

1. Get together with your spouse or partner, and discuss how each of you feels about your adolescent using drugs and alcohol. Try to arrive at a consensus on the issues below by sending and receiving information, brainstorming, and evaluating solutions. This is a good opportunity to apply the problem-solving skills you have learned in previous chapters.
   a. What age is too early to start using tobacco, alcohol, and other drugs?
   b. Where can they be used?
   c. Which substances are dangerous?
2. Draw up a list of house rules that reflect your goals and what your adolescent is doing now. Specify clearly what is allowed and what is not. Set consequences for rule violations and compliance. Write these down.

3. Have a meeting with your adolescent and explain the new rules and consequences. Follow the guidelines for introducing sensitive issues and the rules for family forums.
4. Carefully monitor your adolescent's moods, behavior, activities, and choice of friends.
5. Evaluate your set of rules and consequences, and do some fine-tuning if necessary.

CHAPTER 8

School Problems

It is frustrating to watch from the sidelines as your children struggle in school. Most parents become concerned when they see bad grades on a report card or receive a call from the principal about inappropriate behavior, but they don't know what to do about it. If you have an adolescent with school problems and you have established a reasonable amount of structure at home, this chapter is for you. It describes how you can become involved in turning school failure into a success story. The approach includes establishing and maintaining study routines at home, and designing programs with the school.

There is a great deal of diversity in the situations parents face with respect to school problems. Some adolescents can be hard to get along with at home because they are moody and unwilling to help with routine tasks, but these same youngsters do outstanding work at school. In this case, showing some interest in their activities and a few words of encouragement may be all that is necessary to keep them going. Some children do well in school. Then, for no apparent reason, their grades take a dive, and you are puzzled about how to handle this new state of affairs. This chapter describes the steps you can take to get your adolescent back on track. Still other youngsters have chronic problems with school. Such children usually have a number of other problems as well. If this is true for your adolescent, read *Part 1: The Basics,* and work through each of the step-by-step homework assignments before you try to carry out the suggestions in this chapter. You will have a hard time managing school problems unless you know how to apply the basic techniques.

The majority of the parents in our culture correctly assume that their adolescents will not be going to college. This may be due to a lack of interest, an insufficient grade point average, or the family may not have the money to put their children through college. The parents and adolescents are aware of this, so they tend to downplay the importance of setting goals for academic work. Other parents are convinced that what is taught in high school is of little practical value, so they do not monitor how well their teenagers are doing. This is an unfortunate attitude that is not supported by the research studies that have been completed so far.

Follow-up studies have shown that the skills adolescents learn in high school have a *great deal* of practical value. In high school, adolescents learn how to complete projects, meet deadlines, and fulfill responsibilities. These skills are more critical for surviving in the adult world than the actual content of the courses. Academic achievement in high school also has a dramatic impact on the adolescent's sense of self-worth. It is predictive of success in the world of work, even if college is not a goal. Students who get good grades and high scores on tests feel better about themselves than those who do poorly. A 10-year follow-up study showed that students who learned how to work in high school used those skills later on to acquire and hold better jobs with higher pay.

These practical and psychological considerations suggest that it is important for parents to be involved in helping their children achieve some degree of academic success in school. This does not mean that adolescents must be pushed to get As or Bs on their report cards, but adolescents should be expected to put forth a good effort. Parents can make a difference by helping their children learn important work skills. The simplest and most direct method is for parents to provide structure and support for completing regular homework assignments.

Teachers also make a big difference in how successful students are in school. Cross-cultural studies have shown that the amount of time the teacher and students spend on academic topics is significantly related to how well the children do on achievement tests. It also has been shown that the academic performance of students is higher in schools that require students to do more homework. These results support a strikingly simple explanation of academic achievement—the more time children spend on academic subject matter, the more they learn. This concept is also supported by our own studies of families. The children who receive support at home for completing homework assignments get better grades and higher scores on achievement tests.

Parents with antisocial children do not seem to provide the necessary structure and support for completing homework assignments. These youngsters are good at avoiding responsibilities. One of their favorite ways of dealing with parental concerns about schoolwork is to say they don't have homework or that they finished all of it at school. A quick telephone call to their teachers can verify whether this is true. Most teachers start assigning homework by fourth or fifth grade, particularly in subjects such as math and language arts. If your child "does not have homework," check with the school. Even if there really is no homework, ask the teacher to recommend materials for you to work on together at home. It is easy for busy parents to assume their children are being completely educated at school and that it therefore isn't necessary to be involved in the process. But it is up to you to make sure that your child is learning the core skills and to take action if there is evidence that your child is slipping.

Designing a Homework Routine

There are some basic principles to follow in setting up a homework routine. If your children do well in school, you probably don't have to question their study habits. If they are having trouble, however, it is your responsibility to take the lead and establish a structured study program. Here are some steps to take.

1. Decide how much study time your adolescent should put in on a daily basis. If your adolescent currently does no studying at all, start with a small amount. Fifteen minutes a day is a good beginning because it does not require too much effort. If you start with a step that is too big, you will encounter resistance and the program may fail. For youngsters who already have the discipline to study 15 minutes or more every day, but still have poor grades, add another 15 minutes. Gradually increase the required study time until they are successfully completing their assignments.

2. Provide a good setting for schoolwork. This means a quiet, comfortable place, with adequate lighting, clear working space, and few interruptions. Make this available, even if you have to ask everyone else in the family to be quiet during study time. If you want your children to do well in school, you will find a way no matter how crowded and noisy your home may be. Do not allow siblings or phone calls from friends to interrupt the adolescent during study time.

Youngsters sometimes insist that they can concentrate with the TV on. Unless they are doing well in their schoolwork, do not permit TV, although listening to music on the radio may be all right.

3. Set a regular time when the adolescent goes to the designated place and does his or her homework. This should be the *same* time every day, unless the adolescent's schedule makes it impossible. Many families tell us that it is very difficult to set a regular time because their lives are so chaotic. When parents decide their children's grades are a priority, they find that it *is* possible to organize one part of the day. It might mean setting a regular time for dinner, or it may be necessary for the parents to cut out some of their extra activities. This is a basic commitment that parents must make before the child can learn how to be disciplined about studying. Following a regular routine is important.

The first few weeks might be spent simply teaching the adolescent to go to the study spot at a certain time and sit there for 15 minutes (a detailed example is provided in Chapter 4 of *Part 1: The*

Basics). This may seem silly, but after a while, most youngsters begin to use the time to do their work.

4. Require the adolescent to use this study time five days a week, whether or not there is homework. This approach makes it less tempting for the adolescent to say that there is no homework, because study time is required regardless of whether there is an assignment. There is always some kind of skill-building activity that can be done: practicing spelling; writing short stories, essays, or poetry; practicing an instrument; or reading schoolbooks.

5. Check every so often to make sure the adolescent is following the routine. Don't act like a private investigator when you do this. Be encouraging and pleasant.

Wrong: Mom sneaks up to Hugo's room and suddenly whips open the door. Hugo, who has been staring out of the window, jumps in his chair and snarls something truly unpleasant. An argument ensues.

Better: Mom walks up to Hugo's bedroom and knocks politely. She waits until Hugo responds before opening the door. Then, smiling and using a pleasant tone of voice, she asks, "How are you doing?" Although Hugo frowns and snarls, "Fine!" she smiles again and says, "You've got 20 minutes done—10 more to go," and gently closes the door.

Even if Hugo had been staring out the window, as in the first scene, what he experienced in this second scene was encouragement for taking a step in the right direction (sitting at his desk in his study spot). In the first scene, he was punished for lack of perfection. It is not necessary to sneak up on adolescents; that just makes them more paranoid than they already are.

6. Immediately record the adolescent's study time. Keep a chart in a convenient place and write down the time spent at the study area each day. Demonstrate your respect for the amount of work your adolescent does by recording it right away. Offer praise and encouragement for any work done. Remember that when you use encouragement to foster growth, the changes take place slowly; even though you are making progress toward the final goal, it will take some time to see the results.

7. Try to understand how hard this is for your adolescent. It's not just a rebellious attitude that leads teenagers to avoid schoolwork. It is hard to be disciplined about studying, and it takes effort to learn new material. Youngsters are subjected to criticism from peers and teachers on almost a daily basis, and they often feel ignorant and foolish when they make common mistakes. The learning process is not fun until the adolescent reaches a fairly high level of skill.

8. Make the study routine a pleasant experience. Do not gripe, nag, use guilt, or compare your youngsters with other, more studious and successful children. Accept them as they are, and plan to help them grow a little bit each week. Offer assistance if they need it, and give them as much praise and encouragement as you can. Look for something they are doing right, even if it is just sitting at their desk at the designated time.

9. Provide incentives for following the study routine. Make the reward that is earned worth the youngster's effort. Involve your adolescent in negotiating which rewards would inspire a good effort. Some families use incentives such as money, extra telephone time, permission to go out on a weekend or weeknight, or even use of the family car. Some additional ideas are presented in Chapter 4 of *Part 1: The Basics*. Make sure that you give rewards even for very small successes. The main problem most parents have when starting a study routine is that they expect too much, too fast.

10. Use the "when/then" principle with study time. This means letting your children know that *when* they finish their study time, *then* they can engage in pleasant activities such as watching TV, going out for the evening, and talking on the telephone. According to this principle, it is best to schedule study time as early in the day as possible.

11. Talk to your children about school. Respond to what they say with interest and compassion. Do not treat the exchange as an inquisition. When you tell family members about your day, how do you want *them* to respond? Use the same approach when you discuss what is happening at school with your children. If your adolescent tells you that a teacher is a jerk, don't use this as an opportunity to give a lecture about respecting adults. That's a sure way to turn off the flow of the conversation. If they tell you about a test they failed, be sympathetic. You can give them advice about how to be prepared for tests some other time. It is very important to listen when children tell you about their troubles, without trying to provide solutions. Above all, *take an interest in what they are doing right,* and build on that.

The Case of Hugo the Horrible

Hugo is 16, and by his own declaration he is already an enlightened young man. Since his parents' divorce two years ago, he has become very skilled at arguing by practicing on his mother. During this same period of time, his grades at school have been getting consistently worse. Hugo is also beginning to assert that he should be allowed to drop out of school because it is a waste of time. These statements are not accompanied by any mention of getting a job and making a living. His verbal attacks on his mother cover every aspect of her life except the fact that she has a good job and pays for all of his daily needs. Hugo also has unrestricted access to the family car.

Act I: You Have Nothing to Lose but the Car

The Scene. Hugo's mother has just finished doing the dishes. The action begins as she walks into the living room, where Hugo is lying on the couch watching TV.

Mother: Remember, Hugo, when that program is over, we are scheduled to have a family meeting.

Hugo: (groaning and waving her away) I don't think there's anything I need to talk about, so let's forget it.

Later, when the program is finished, Mom walks in again and turns the TV off. As she sits down in the chair next to Hugo, she smiles and leans forward to plug in the small audiotape recorder. Then she begins the discussion.

Mother: I called the school about the report card that you said you couldn't find. I found out that you earned a D+ average last term. You used to be a good student until the last year or two. I'm concerned, and I want to help you get back on track again.

Hugo: The teachers are jerks, so who cares about their grades? Everyone knows that my school has the worst teachers in the country. I showed you some of the books they want us to read—it's kid stuff. Only nerds take that junk seriously. And besides, I don't really want to talk about this right now. (Hugo gets up and starts to put on his shoes.)

Mother: I'm afraid it's not up to you. Nobody can make you *like* school, but it's your job to learn what they have to teach you. I've decided that I'm going to support you for doing good schoolwork, and I'm going to help you establish a regular time for studying from now on.

Hugo: (staring hard at his mother, then sneering) And just *how* do you think you're going to do that? Are you gonna sit at my desk and take notes for me, or what?

Mother: Well, for starters you're going to have to study 15 minutes a day if you want to use the car on weekends.

Hugo: (his mouth hanging open in astonishment) Yeah, what about the car? You don't even take care of it—you run all over town with no oil in it. What do you care about the car?

Mother: That's not the point—we can talk about oil later if you'd like. Right now there is the problem of earning car privileges on weekends by doing your homework each night. Not doing homework means no car.

Hugo: (looking flustered now) But I don't *have* any homework. The little bit they give me, I finish during study hall. Only idiots have to study at home.

Mother: When I heard about your grades, I talked to your teachers. Several of them said the reason you do poorly is that you don't turn in your assignments. It's up to you to keep track of your assignments and bring them home. I want to see them each night. I'm not going to correct them, but I want to see you doing homework for 15 minutes each day.

Hugo: I already told you, *I don't have any homework!* This is just great! Now my home is turning into some kind of prison camp. You want me to do a bunch of busy work—is that going to make you happy?

Mother: Write down your assignments and bring them home. I called your math and geography teachers. They both told me you have daily assignments. If you study for 15 minutes each day, you can have the car on Friday or Saturday night. If you show me your work each day as well, you can use it on both nights. Otherwise, you won't be allowed to use the car on the weekends.

Hugo: You can take your damn car and shove it. (Hugo storms out of the room and slams the door behind him.)

Commentary

In terms of problem-solving skills, Hugo earns another D. Mom gets an A, however, for controlling her emotions. The situation at school had deteriorated to a point where it would be difficult to have a pleasant family discussion about grades no matter what approach Hugo's mother tried. In an exchange like this, it isn't necessary (or realistic) to emerge victorious by defeating the irritable adolescent. Hugo's mother made the right choice in not trying to stop him from leaving the room; there was no reason for her to run after him. Her goal was to set a new process in motion—that is, establishing a routine for studying. When Hugo became abusive, she played her trump card, which was the keys to the car. After she makes it clear to Hugo that there are changes in the wind, she can carry out her plan one step at a time. First, Hugo will have to learn that she means business; he will not have access to the car if he doesn't work within the system. He can't avoid dealing with the situation for too long because the weekend is just around the corner, and it will cramp his style if he doesn't negotiate an agreement with his mother about homework. At some deeper level, Hugo probably realizes that he is being outrageous in ignoring his schoolwork. It is interesting to note that when children like Hugo get older, they often say that they wish their parents had made them do better in school. Letting them get away with something as blatant as failing in school communicates to children that you don't care about them. Even though they will fight you tooth and nail, everyone benefits if you take responsibility for changing the situation.

Act II: The Great Compromise

The Scene. When the weekend rolled around, Hugo's mother announced that the keys to the car would not be available until Hugo signed an agreement about the homework issue. Because she thought Hugo might have his own keys, she did not tempt him by leaving the car at home. She parked it at an unnamed friend's house on Friday evening when she stayed home, and she took the car with her on Saturday evening when she went out. After a weekend with no car, Hugo called for an emergency meeting.

Hugo: (smiling confidently as he sits on the couch) I don't agree with you on the school thing. There isn't anything they have to teach me that's worth a pinch of s**t. They just don't know how to get kids interested. But I'll tell you what. Let me prove I can do it. If I don't get a B average next term, then take the keys away. (He leans back triumphantly.)

Mother: (She nods her head and smiles.) That's encouraging, but you promised that last term, too, and it didn't seem to work out. Now I'm sticking to my original offer—no homework means no car. When do you want to start doing your homework regularly?

Hugo: I already told you—*I don't have any!*

Mother: Then talk to the teachers of the subjects that you are flunking, and ask them for makeup assignments. It's your problem. You work it out. Where will you do the homework?

Hugo: Right here on the couch.

Mother: Well, that probably isn't a good idea because the TV is right in front of you. I want to make it clear that there will be no TV at night until after your homework is done. I think the table in your room would be better—there are fewer distractions there, and it is easier to work when you are sitting at a table. Do you want a desk instead? We could find one at a second-hand store.

Hugo: The table is OK. But how much time do I have to spend doing homework every night before I can use the car on the weekends?

Mother: I know it's hard for you, so let's keep it short for the first week or two. How about 15 minutes a day, Monday through Friday, for starters?

Hugo: (His hands are jammed deep into his jacket pockets, and he is staring at the floor.) OK, I guess that's fair enough.

Commentary

Notice again that Mom ignored Hugo's inappropriate behavior in negotiating the homework issue. She didn't dock him for having a bad attitude and swearing; in fact, she didn't even label it. Instead, she remained steadfast in her mission to engage him in a study routine by using the most valuable resource she has—the car!

There are a couple of interesting points about this exchange that should be noted. For one thing, Hugo cleverly used the "when/then" principle in an attempt to delay the loss of the car. Children sometimes seem to understand this principle better than their parents. But Mom was very good at sidestepping distractions, including this one. She quickly turned down his proposal and stayed on target by asking where the studying would be done. This illustrates another surprising quality of teenagers. They may *say* they will never comply, but if you calmly proceed by asking how they will carry out the needed change, they negotiate those details as though their refusal had never been spoken.

Hugo called a meeting the following week. During the meeting, he pointed out that it wasn't always fair to hold him to the original agreement to do homework five nights a week. The issue came up because this week family friends had come over to visit Wednesday night, making it impossible for him to do his homework. His mother agreed that in certain cases like this it would be all right for him to make up the homework some other time. Hugo's mother was impressed by the fact that for the first time in months Hugo was making an effort to study. Giving in on this small point was a good way to show Hugo that she could be reasonable. Hugo made up the 15 minutes on Saturday morning so that he could use the car to go to the football game. Hugo was pleased that he was able to work within the system to get what he wanted, and his mother was happy to see him doing homework. Hugo was successful in following the studying routine for several weeks, and his mother gradually increased the daily requirement to 30 minutes. Hugo's mother also negotiated an agreement with him to do some chores to earn money for gas and other things. When the next report card came out, almost every teacher mentioned that Hugo's homework assignments were coming in on time. Overall, he received a C+ average. This was an improvement over the situation just a few months ago.

The next problem that surfaced concerned Hugo's behavior at school. His teachers were impressed that he was doing some work, but Hugo was still skipping classes occasionally, and when he was there, he often had a rotten attitude. This new problem meant that his mother had to put more effort into monitoring Hugo's daily progress at school. To do this, she used a school card. This technique requires the youngster to carry a card to each class and get it signed by the teachers with a brief evaluation of targeted behaviors. The next section describes how to set up a school-card program.

Monitoring School Behavior

Monitoring school behavior becomes necessary when your efforts at home don't solve the whole problem. This is the case when homework assignments are not turned in (even though they may have been completed), classes are skipped, tardiness is common-place, or there are behavior problems. Most parents wonder why the teachers and counselors at school cannot resolve these problems. If the problems are persistent, however, the most effective approach is for parents and school personnel to work together. This is an extension of the idea that parents need to present a unified front to children. The school card helps to link the parent and the school in their efforts to make significant changes in behavior and academic performance. The card provides the parents with daily information about their adolescent's progress in school. Here are the steps for setting up a school-card program.

1. Contact the school. Call the school and ask to speak to the teacher who has primary responsibility for your adolescent. Make an appointment with that teacher, explaining that you want to become involved in helping your youngster do better. Find out what problems your adolescent is having. Don't be defensive. Use your best listening skills and paraphrase what the teacher is saying. Treat this as another kind of problem-solving session. If you communicate your interest and concern, most teachers will try to help.

2. Suggest using a school card. Explain that you want a simple way to monitor your adolescent's daily progress in school. Say that you would like your child to carry a card to each class and obtain evaluations for one or two of the problem behaviors that the teacher has described. Let the teacher know that you don't expect school personnel to do anything more than simply provide a brief evaluation accompanied by their signature. Explain that it will be the youngster's responsibility to present the card for evaluation.

Most schools will cooperate with this approach. In fact, many schools use this same system for students who are having trouble. Unfortunately, some schools will resist the idea. Talk to the school counselor or principal if the homeroom teacher is not cooperative. Ask for some suggestions to help you learn about your child's school behavior so that you can provide appropriate consequences. Try not to be angry or hostile because this will shut the door on any possibility of organizing a cooperative effort, and your youngster will be the one who loses.

3. Design a school card. Based on the problems described, include one or two behaviors for teachers to evaluate. Most families are concerned with behavior that falls into one of three categories: on time/tardy, classroom behavior, and assignments complete/incomplete. It is not necessary to use the card for attendance, because a signature cannot be obtained by an absent child. An example of a school card is provided in the homework assignment for this chapter.

The adolescent carries this card to every class and is responsible for obtaining each teacher's evaluation and signature at the end of class. Failure to bring the card home fully signed, regardless of the reason (including "losing" the card, forgetfulness, or other catastrophes) results in loss of some small, but regular privilege for that day only (for example, use of the telephone, permission to go out, use of the TV or radio). Bringing the card home with signatures earns a daily reward as negotiated with the youngster. Don't let the adolescent convince you that the teacher simply forgot to sign it; the card is not the teacher's responsibility, it is the adolescent's.

4. Introduce the school-card procedure to the adolescent. Tell your youngster that you have been in touch with the school because you are concerned with specific problems, and outline what these are (tardiness, incomplete assignments, classroom behavior, etc.). Say that you want to help solve these problems by supporting successful behavior. Explain the procedure: the adolescent will carry the card to each class; at the end of class, the adolescent will ask the teacher to evaluate his or her behavior and sign the card. Negotiate what the reward will be for bringing the card home signed. Make sure that the reward is something the child values, because this is asking a lot from your child.

5. Start small. In the beginning, don't require good marks on the card to earn the reward. The first step is to teach your youngster to be responsible about bringing the signed card home by providing a reward. Require a few signatures at first, and gradually increase what your child must do to earn the reward. As in everything else, it is important to take small steps toward the goal.

6. Gradually require good evaluations for rewards. After your adolescent has learned to bring home the signed card regularly, require positive evaluations. If the typical report has about 50% good marks, set the reward standard at 60% for a week or so. As the youngster shows improvement, take another tiny step toward your long-term goal.

7. Use backup rewards to improve the effort. You may want to double the motivation for the adolescent to follow through with the study routine and the school-card program by adding a weekly bonus to the daily rewards. The weekly bonus should be earned for obtaining some percentage of success on both programs. For example, if your child completes 80% of the required studying and brings home good marks on the school card about 60% of the time, set the standard for the weekly reward slightly above these levels.

Key Ideas in This Chapter

1. It is important for parents to monitor their adolescent's performance in school. If there are problems, it is the parents' responsibility to take action.
2. Instead of focusing on grades, begin by working on developing a studying routine for your adolescent at home. Good grades will follow later.
3. Gradually increase the criteria for rewards as your adolescent's performance improves.
4. If there are problems at school, work with school personnel to resolve them.

Chapter Eight Homework Assignment

1. Evaluate your adolescent's current study habits. Is there a good place in your home for studying? Is there a regular time? How much time is spent studying on a regular basis? Make up your own chart, or use the one provided.
2. If homework is a problem, design a study-habit program following the guidelines provided in the beginning of the chap-

ter. Explain it to your youngster and begin recording the daily behavior.

3. Once you have this well under way (that is, your adolescent is consistently spending time in the study place), contact the school to find out about other problems that may need to be addressed. If there are problems, set up a school-card program.

Steps for Designing a Homework Routine

1. Decide how much study time your adolescent should put in on a daily basis.
2. Provide a good setting for schoolwork.
3. Set a regular time when the adolescent goes to the designated place and does his or her homework.
4. Require the adolescent to use this study time five days a week whether or not there is homework.
5. Check every so often to make sure the adolescent is following the routine.
6. Immediately record the adolescent's study time.
7. Try to understand how hard this is for your adolescent.
8. Make the study routine a pleasant experience.
9. Provide incentives for following the study routine.
10. Use the "when/then" principle with study time.
11. Talk to your children about school.

Steps for Setting Up a School-Card Program

1. Contact the school.
2. Suggest using a school card.
3. Design a school card.
4. Introduce the school-card procedure to the adolescent.
5. Start small.
6. Gradually require good evaluations for rewards.
7. Use backup rewards to improve the effort.

Study Time Chart

	Time Spent Studying				
	Mon	Tues	Wed	Th	Fri
Week 1					
Week 2					
Week 3					
Week 4					

From *Parents and Adolescents Living Together: Part 2—Family Problem Solving* (2nd ed.) © 2005 by M. S. Forgatch and G. R. Patterson. Champaign, IL: Research Press (800-519-2707; www.researchpress.com).

School Card

Period		Mon	Tues	Wed	Thurs	Fri
1	Behav.					
	Assign.					
2	Behav.					
	Assign.					
3	Behav.					
	Assign.					
4	Behav.					
	Assign.					
5	Behav.					
	Assign.					
6	Behav.					
	Assign.					
7	Behav.					
	Assign.					

Behavior

1 = Poor

2 = Acceptable

3 = Good

Assignments

C = Complete

I = Incomplete

From *Parents and Adolescents Living Together: Part 2—Family Problem Solving* (2nd ed.) © 2005 by M. S. Forgatch and G. R. Patterson. Champaign, IL: Research Press (800-519-2707; www.researchpress.com).

Glossary

Active listening means paying attention to what your children say. When your adolescent daughter says she had a bad day at school, you should stop what you are doing and get into her world for a while. Be sympathetic, and ask for more details in an unobtrusive way. Active listening refers to being involved in what your children are saying rather than being passive and uninterested. Offering advice is not part of active listening.

Antisocial behavior is experienced as aversive by others, and it has a negative social impact (that is, there is a victim). For example, teasing, disobedience, and fighting are antisocial behaviors.

The term **backup** has both general and specific meanings. Generally, it refers to the follow-up consequences that parents impose to provide support for the positive or negative sanctions they use with adolescents. In this mini-series, the term **backup reward** means providing a weekly bonus if the teenager reaches the daily criterion a certain number of days per week on the point chart (this is discussed in detail in Chapter 5 of *Part 1: The Basics*). A **backup punishment** means adding a negative consequence, such as privilege removal, if the teenager refuses to do a five-minute work chore that has already been assigned as punishment. (This is described in detail in Chapter 6 of *Part 1: The Basics.*)

Brainstorming is the process of generating as many ideas as possible.

Coercion means using unpleasant behaviors to get what you want. Family members who use disagreeable behaviors such as nagging or yelling to teach other family members to start doing something (or to strengthen a behavior) are involved in the coercion process. Coercion derives its ability to change behavior through the contingent presentation of unpleasant events. The following is an example of how coercion is used in families: An adolescent son is asked to mow the lawn; the boy's response is to throw a tantrum; his parents respond by giving in instead of requiring him to do the work. In this example, the boy has taught his parents to give in when he throws a tantrum. The net result is that the boy "wins."

Compliance refers to whether children carry out the requests and commands their parents make. Compliance also implies a willingness to cooperate and follow rules.

A **contingent** arrangement implies a "when/then" connection between the adolescent's behavior and the parent's response. When the adolescent comes home late, a work chore is imposed; when the adolescent takes care of certain responsibilities, specific privileges are earned.

The **family forum** is a highly structured family meeting.

Irritability is testy, angry, or hostile behavior.

Monitoring refers to how well parents keep track of their adolescents' behavior away from home. In order to be effective as parents, it is necessary to know the answers to the four basic questions: Who will your children be with? Where are they? What are they doing? When will they be home?

The phrase **"pain control"** refers to the use of extremely unpleasant responses by family members to control the behavior of others.

The term **process** is used to describe changes that take place slowly, over time. For example, aging is a process; it is difficult to notice the changes from one day to the next, but after several years the changes are obvious.

Punishment is somewhat like coercion in that the key element is the contingent presentation of unpleasant events. The difference is that, in punishment sequences, these events decrease or weaken behaviors. The following is an example of how punishment is used in families: A father tells his adolescent daughter that she must finish her homework before she does anything else; the daughter does homework for five minutes and then calls her best friend on the telephone; the father hears her using the telephone and interrupts the call; he tells his daughter that she has just lost her telephone privileges for the day. In this example, the father used punishment to teach his daughter to stop engaging in distracting activities when she is supposed to be doing her homework.

A (positive) **reinforcer** is defined in terms of its effect on behavior. When a reinforcer follows a behavior, the behavior is strengthened. This is a contingent arrangement. A reinforcer is an event or thing that feels good to the person receiving it.

Social reinforcers are found in the behavior of other people. A smile, a nod of approval, or words of encouragement are examples of social reinforcers. **Nonsocial reinforcers,** on the other hand, are not derived from the behavior of other people. They are desirable things or events such as rewards, money, and privileges that can be used to strengthen behavior. (They are also called "tangible rewards" because they tend to be visible events or things.)

Socialization is the process of teaching children about the rules of society and how to respond appropriately to the people around them. Interacting directly with parents and other people is the primary vehicle for socialization, but children also learn vicariously by watching people interact with one another. Well-socialized children tend to follow the rules in a given setting, they are liked by their peers, and are socially responsive. The **readiness to be socialized** refers to how receptive children are to learning new behaviors and skills from others.

The concept of treating someone (usually a family member) with the same courtesy you would extend to a stranger is referred to as the **stranger rule.**

Tracking means paying attention to specific adolescent behaviors. It involves breaking global concepts such as "bad attitude" into components that everyone can recognize.